German Aircraft and Armament

OFFICE OF THE
ASSISTANT CHIEF OF AIR STAFF, INTELLIGENCE
WASHINGTON, D.C.

German Aircraft and Armament

INFORMATIONAL INTELLIGENCE

SUMMARY No. 44-32

October 1944

(Replaces No. 43-33, all copies of which should be destroyed)

Distribution: SQUADRONS

Brassey's
Washington, D.C.

First published by the U.S. Army Air Forces in 1944.

Published by Brassey's in 2000.

ISBN 1-57488-291-0   (alk. paper)

Printed in Canada on acid-free paper that meets the
American National Standards Institute Z39-48 Standard.

Brassey's, Inc.
22841 Quicksilver Drive
Dulles, Virginia 20166

First Edition

10   9   8   7   6   5   4   3   2   1

Foreword

The startling importance of this volume must be understood in terms of the incredible advances in the operations of the U.S. Army Air Forces intelligence system after 1941 and in light of the spotty history of American intelligence work in the field of aviation prior to that time.

The United States was first faced with the problem of gathering intelligence on foreign air services during World War I. When the United States entered that war on April 6, 1917, fighting in the air had been going on for thirty-two months. The air forces of both the Allies and the Central Powers had grown in strength and capability, with thousands of aircraft deployed in fighting squadrons on virtually every front. Immense industries had grown up to manufacture the aircraft, and huge training establishments were turning out pilots, observers, and gunners.

In painful contrast, the U.S. Army Air Service had about fifty-five aircraft in April 1917, none of which were remotely suitable for combat. There was virtually no aviation industry, a minimum training base, and very little inclination to expand such, despite the fact that American airmen had been fighting in both the French air service (some as members of the Lafayette Escadrille) and the Royal Flying Corps. Incredibly, the U.S. Army had no basis on which to make decisions about procuring aircraft from either American or foreign sources. It had absolutely no knowledge of the enemy's aircraft, except that which might be obtained from the pages of *The Aeroplane*, the remarkable British publication that was light years ahead of any American magazine in terms of objective content.

The United States attempted to remedy the situation by force-feeding the indigenous industry with the $640 million in funds suddenly available from Congress and by sending commissions abroad to study foreign aircraft and recommend which should be built in the United States. The first of these, the Bolling Commission, came back with a laundry list of recommendations that included building the de Havilland D.H.-4, the SPAD XIII, the Handley Page 0/400, and the Caproni bomber. At the same time, American manufacturers were putting forward their own designs. Few of these were of acceptable quality, and none would be manufactured in time to see service overseas. Ultimately, American units would fly aircraft produced by foreign governments, with the sole exception of those units that were supplied with the British-designed but American-built de Havilland DH-4s. (Curiously, the designation was changed from the British de Havilland D. H. 4 to the American de Havilland DH-4.) The American DH-4s were equipped with the Liberty engine, which, with the Curtiss flying boats and trainers, may be said to be the greatest contribution of the American aviation industry to the war.

As the war progressed, information on the air war, particularly on enemy aircraft, flowed to the United States, where it was collected and analyzed at McCook Field, Ohio. At war's end, a large selection of enemy aircraft were brought to McCook Field and tested, then stored in rather tatty buildings, awaiting display in an air service museum. Photos of the period show long rows of German aircraft fuselages, some with engines, some without, their wings stored elsewhere. Sadly, these were all scrapped, well before the period when enthusiasts would have clamored for their restoration.

With the postwar cutbacks, intelligence gathering was almost abandoned except for the efforts of American air attachés. Many of these reports, especially those of John J. Ide, were remarkably comprehensive and could have served as a clear signal that Germany was rearming. Capt. Truman Smith, an attaché in Berlin, was so concerned that he lobbied successfully for Charles A. Lindbergh to visit Germany and be shown the strengths of the nascent Luftwaffe. Another major American aviator, the former Navy racing pilot Alford Williams, also wrote about the extent of German rearmament.

Both Lindbergh and Williams toured Europe and made valuable and generally accurate assessments of the air forces of France, Great Britain, and Germany. (Lindbergh's report has been attacked in recent years as being overoptimistic about Germany's capabilities, but his comments were basically correct.) Unfortunately even the reports of such celebrities were ignored. The important fact is that an adequate American intelligence service would have been able to gain significant information from their reports.

The sad truth is that at the time there was an unfortunate disposition on the part of the U.S. Army and, to an even greater degree, the American public, to underestimate the capability of foreign designers and to believe with a naive chauvinism in the superiority of American designers. This was not a simple, charming national foible, for it had direct and adverse results on any attempt to induce Congress to appropriate a reasonable amount of money for self-defense. The chauvinism was particularly harmful in regard to the Japanese, who were regarded as mere copyists who could neither build good airplanes nor find good pilots to fly them. The pilots were believed to be myopic, with a substantial overbite!

Unfortunately, just as the reports from observers in France and the experience of members of the Lafayette Escadrille were ignored in 1917, so were the hard-edged assessments of Japanese air power put forward by no less a personality than Claire Chennault. The contemptuous dismissal of Japanese capability would be reversed after Pearl Harbor, when Japanese planes and pilots were suddenly endowed with exaggerated capabilities.

The problems in American air intelligence were not unknown. In 1938, when then Maj. Gen. Henry H. Arnold became commanding general of the Army Air Corps, he wrote that "the weakest area in the entire air program is the air intelligence organization." He blamed this in part on the lack of cooperation from the War Department G-2 section, but also on the failure of the Air Corps to recognize the need to develop its own system of intelligence.

In the fall of 1939, Arnold sent Lt. Col. Carl Spaatz and Maj. George C. Kenney to Europe as combat observers. They prepared many accurate reports that affected Air Corps plans and preparations. In August 1940, more observers were sent, including first lieutenants Herbert "Hub" Zemke and John Alison. They were impressed with the British system of operations, a sentiment that was confirmed when Brig. Gen. Ira Eaker and his staff made a study of RAF Bomber Command in February and March 1942. First the Eighth Air Force, then the Army Air Forces as a whole were reorganized along RAF lines.

Fortunately, the brilliant creators of Air War Plan Division-1, Lieutenant Colonels Harold L. George, Kenneth N. Walker, Laurence S. Kuter, and Haywood S. Hansell, Jr., all future general officers, had direct access to RAF intelligence and prepared their amazingly accurate forecast accordingly. This began a pattern that would continue through the war, by which the U.S. Army Air Forces intelligence officers would both adopt British methods and use British capability.

The results of those efforts may be seen in this remarkable compendium of intelligence, *German Aircraft and Armament*, which was first published in October 1944. This intelligence guidebook was issued down to the squadron level. While much of this data is now available from postwar sources, there is much in this book that is not represented in later publications. By reading the material carefully, one can also spot where incorrect inferences were being made, as in the additional technical data on the Heinkel He 219, which suggests that a ventral turbo-jet unit was sometimes fitted, giving a top speed of 450 mph.

Much of the material derived from the extensive testing done by the British (and to a far lesser degree, by the French) of captured German aircraft. My old friend Capt. Eric M. "Winkle" Brown became chief test pilot of the Royal Aircraft Establishment at Farnborough in January 1944, where he commanded the elite Aerodynamics Flight. There, with many other highly skilled pilots, he flew the captured German aircraft.

Testing was rigorous and often done in direct competition with contemporary British types in order to be sure that the data was accurate. Contrary to all the prewar propaganda that had implied German aircraft were made of ersatz materials and with poor manufacturing techniques, Brown and the other pilots found them to be remarkably well-built machines, logically designed and suited for their intended purpose.

Similar tests were conducted at the USAAF's Wright Field in Ohio, and similar conclusions were drawn. One of the most revealing studies occurred when a Messerschmitt Bf 110 was sent to the Vultee Aircraft Company for analysis. There it was found that while there were no luxuries in the design and construction of the Bf 110, it was a sensible, well-made machine from which American designers could learn much.

It is interesting to compare the performance or dimension statistics in this volume with those in generally accepted modern reference sources. They are generally remarkably close, almost always within 3 or 4 percent of each other. The Messerschmitt Bf 109F-4, for example, is given a maximum speed of 395 mph at 22,000 feet in this manual, compared to the 388 mph at 21,325 feet quoted in William Green's fine work, *The Warplanes of the Third Reich*. Sometimes, however, the intelligence estimates falter. The Heinkel He 177, termed a twin "doubled" engine bomber, has its speed estimated with real accuracy but is given a range of only 3,000 miles with a full fuel load and no bombs. Green cites a range of 3,100 miles even when encumbered with two Fritz-X missiles carried externally.

An amazing variety of aircraft are found within the fifty-seven types presented in *German Aircraft and Armament*, ranging from such standards as the Focke Wulf Fw 190 to the unorthodox, asymmetric Blohm & Voss BV 141B to a license-built (by both Aero and Avia) Czechoslovakian B-71 version of the Soviet Union's Tupelov SB-2.

Where *German Aircraft and Armament* excels is in the details it presents that are found in few (if any) other sources. At the time, it offered valuable information to those flying combat; today, it provides invaluable information to researchers and enthusiasts. One important example is the field-of-fire diagrams. These clearly show how inadequate the armament was on many of the German bombers, particularly such workhorses as the Heinkel He 111.

Even more arcane figures are quoted for those who really delve into performance characteristics. These include such things as propeller diameters (a rarely found dimension, yet critical for evaluating performance), supercharger ratios, impeller diameters, compression ratios, fuel octane requirements, and many more. One unusual but informative bit of information is that horsepower ratings are given at specific rpm and manifold pressure settings, information not usually found outside of pilot's manuals.

As might be expected for an October 1944 publication, there is far less accurate data on such advanced types as the Messerschmitt Me 163 or Me 262, or the Heinkel He 280. While reasonably accurate top speed figures are given for the two Messerschmitt aircraft, there is nothing recorded for the Heinkel jet, no doubt because its testing was far more limited than that of the other two. What is interesting are the speculations the intelligence people permitted themselves. For example, they note that the Me 163 "lands on skid which probably incorporates a braking device." It did have a braking device, of course: friction.

Hard data on these and other aircraft would be gathered for several years. Wright Field was the scene of tremendous progress in all aspects of intelligence work, and it evolved rapidly during the war. A specialized Foreign Equipment Branch was ultimately established. One of the major sources for foreign equipment resulted from the remarkable accomplishments of Col. (later Maj. Gen.) Harold E. Watson, whose "Watson's Whizzers" gathered up the latest aircraft and equipment from Germany even as the war was ending. The U.S. Navy also tested captured enemy aircraft all during the war and established a counterpart to Wright Field's test activities at the Patuxent River Naval Air Station in Maryland.

German Aircraft and Armament provides many levels of entrancing detail, and it is well worth reading the "Additional Technical Data" sections closely, for they include some gems. A reference is made, for example, to the "deck-landing" Messerschmitt Bf 109T, and there is a section devoted to its shipmate, the Fiesler Fi 167. Indirect references are made to *schraege musik* ("jazz music") installations, by which cannons fire forward and upward, although the German term itself is not used. In the same way, references are made to rocket projector tubes mounted both parallel and vertical to wing surfaces. In the Ju 88C-6, a comment is made that "four cement blocks are carried in the rear fuselage as ballast." It is noted that the Messerschmitt Bf 109G series incorporates the use of wood and plywood to save metals, that it has ultra-violet cockpit lighting, and that its oxygen flow is automatically controlled by a barometric capsule. All in all, splendid reading for the buff!

Relatively few *German Aircraft and Armament* manuals were published, and even fewer survive. I had never seen any until my old friend, the scholarly collector Glen Sweeting, showed me the one he had acquired in 1945 at a display of captured German equipment near his home in Canoga Park, California. Glen, perhaps the world's leading expert on German military memorabilia, was already collecting at the age of sixteen. He continues to do so today, thank goodness, and it is from his extensive private collection that this book was reproduced.

Walter J. Boyne
Ashburn, Virginia

OFFICE OF THE
ASSISTANT CHIEF OF AIR STAFF, INTELLIGENCE

Distribution: SQUADRONS.   WASHINGTON, D. C., *October, 1944.*

GERMAN AIRCRAFT AND ARMAMENT
Introduction

This booklet is compiled to present in tabular form technical information at present available concerning currently operational types of German aircraft, together with the armament they carry. In addition, the best available photographs and silhouettes are shown, approximate fields of fire being indicated on the latter. A brief description of each aircraft is given.

A standard form is used to describe the technical data as now known. Supplementary information will be disseminated in Informational Intelligence Summaries, under the heading "Notes On Enemy Aircraft". This additional data should be transcribed into this Summary, either on the current sheets or on the blank forms at the end of each classification.

Individual aircraft are classified according to general use and are arranged in alphabetical and numerical order in each group. By numbering sheets in allotments of 100 to each group, provision is made for adding newly recorded types at the end of their proper classification in the general index.

Information has been obtained from sources believed reliable, but is incomplete in the case of certain aircraft. Further data on all aircraft are urgently desired, particularly with reference to new or unfamiliar models.

THE AIRCRAFT SHOWN ON THE FRONT COVER IS THE ME 109G

INDEX

FIGHTERS

BOMBERS

RECONNAISSANCE AND ARMY COOPERATION

TRANSPORTS AND GLIDER TUGS

NAVAL AND MARINE

GLIDERS

Calculation of Ranges and Speeds

1. The method of assessing "RANGES" is based on the following convention:

    a. Ranges given are ideal still-air ranges. No reduction is made for operational tactics or allowance made for navigational errors, head winds, etc.

    b. Allowance is made for warming up and take-off equivalent to five minutes running at take-off power.

    c. A further allowance is made for the fuel used during climb to the operational altitude at the maximum rate of climb.

    d. The distance covered during the climb is credited to the range but no credit is given for gliding in at the end of the journey.

2. Ranges given opposite the heading "Typical tactical speeds" in the range tables are included to supply idealized estimates of the approximate ranges which may be expected of each aircraft in tactical service under varying conditions of load and fuel. These ranges are based on a set of assumed factors approximating favorable operational conditions: warm-up, taxiing, run-up, take-off and landing equal to ten minutes at maximum rated power; time to climb to rated altitude at maximum continuous power, with allowance for distance covered in climb; time at economical cruising power to within 100 miles of the target, which may be taken as the point of optimum operational distance from base, and 150 miles returning; fifteen minutes of combat at maximum rated power; plus remainder of time and distance available at maximum continuous power under the specified bomb and fuel load. It is emphasized that figures submitted opposite this heading apply only to the one set of typical conditions assumed above. Any variation in conditions would necessitate recalculation of the tactical ranges to meet the specific problem.

3. Speeds shown under "PERFORMANCE" are those with normal fuel load and bombs, if any.

4. Cruising speeds given are average speeds.

DO 217J

DESCRIPTION

The Do 217J is the currently-operational night fighter version of the Do 217 bomber.

The aircraft is a twin-engine, shoulder-wing monoplane. Wing tapers moderately to rounded tips. Slotted ailerons and split flaps are fitted. Nose is metal-panelled. Aft portion of fuse-lage is rounded. There are twin fins and rudders with a slot down the leading edge of each fin to improve control when flying on one engine. Landing gear retracts rearward into engine nacelles; tailwheel retracts. No diving brakes are fitted.

DO 217 J

TWIN ENGINE NIGHT FIGHTER

Mfr. __DORNIER_____ Crew __THREE_____

Duty __NIGHT FIGHTING, INTRUDER, GROUND ATTACK_____

PERFORMANCE

Max. emergency speeds __285__ m. p. h. @ S. L.; __328__ m. p. h. @ __20,000__ ft. alt.; _____ m. p. h. @ _____ ft.alt.

Max. continuous speeds _____ m. p. h. @ S. L.; _____ m. p. h. @ _____ ft. alt.; _____ m. p. h. @ _____ ft. alt.

Cruising speeds: Normal __280__ m. p. h.; ____ economical __210__ m. p. h.; ____ each at __18,000__ ft. altitude.

Climb: To __18,000__ ft. alt. in __13.8__ min.; rate _____ ft./min. at _____ ft. altitude.

Service ceilings: Normal load __29,000__ ft.; max. bomb/fuel load __25,500__ ft.; min. fuel/no bombs __33,000__ ft.

Fuel: { U. S. gal.: Normal __783__ ; max. __1289__ Take-off, in calm air _____ ft.

{ Imp. gal.: Normal __650__ ; max. __1070__ Take-off, over 50 ft. obstacle _____ ft.

RANGES

Speeds	With Normal Fuel/Bomb Load __783__ U. S. gal. and __—__ lb. bombs	With Max. Bomb Load and __1091__ U. S. gal.	With Max. Fuel Load and __—__ lb. Bombs
Economical cruising speed	@ 210 mph - 1250 miles	@ 230 mph-1645 miles	@ 230 mph-1975 miles
Normal cruising speed	@ 280 mph - 1180 miles	@ 275 mph-1635 miles	@ 275 mph-1965 miles
Maximum continuous speed	miles	miles	miles
*Typical tactical speeds	760 miles	980 miles	1,240 miles

*Ref.: p. 4. Para. 2.

POWER PLANT

No. engines __2__ , rated 1755 / 1530 hp., each at __20,000__ ft. alt., with 3,250 / 2,700 r. p. m. and 2,700 / 41.0 in. Hg. __41.0__

Description __BMW 801 D, 14-cylinder, twin-row, air-cooled radial__

Specifications	Supercharger	Propeller	Fuel
Bore __6.14__ in. Dry Wgt. __2960__ lbs.	No. Speeds __2__	Mfr. __V.D.M.__	Rating __100__ octane
Stroke __6.14__ in. Red. Gear __.541__	No. Stages	No. Blades __3__	Inlet System:
Displ. __2550__ cu. in. Eng. Diam. __52__ in.	Ratios __5.31__ ; __8.32__	Diam. __10__ ft., __10__ in.	__Direct__
Comp. Ratio __7 : 1__ Eng. Length ____ in.	Impeller Diam. __13.25__ in.	Pitch Control	__Injection__

ARMAMENT

(F—fixed. M—free.)

For'd fuselage __4x7.9mm, 1000 rpg__
+ __4x20mm, 250 rpg (F)__

For'd wings _____

Through hub _____
Dorsal __1x13mm, 500 rds (M)__
Lateral _____
Ventral __1x13mm (M)__
Tail _____

BOMB/FREIGHT LOAD

Normal load _____ kg., _____ lb.
Max. load __400__ kg., __880__ lb.
Typical stowage
__8x50 kg (110 lbs.)__
__(Can be released individually)__
Alternate stowage _____
_____
_____
Freight _____ lb.
Troops _____

ARMOR

Frontal __Bulkhead, 9mm__
Windshield __armored__
Pilot's seat __armored__

Dorsal __armored__
Lateral __armored__
Ventral __armored__
Bulkhead __armored__

Engine _____

SPECIFICATIONS

Materials __Metal, stressed skin__

Span __62'-5"__ Length __58'__ Height (est) __12'-6"__ Gross wing area __610 sq. ft.__ Tail span _____

Weights: Landing __22,000__ lb.; normal load __27,500__ lb.; max. load __31,500__ lb.

ADDITIONAL TECHNICAL DATA

Possibly 1x30mm forward firing cannon may be fitted. Bomb load only carried on long-range intruder missions. Center part of fuselage and wing unit modified to take 307 U.S. gal. jettisonable tank. No provision made for jettisonable external wing tanks but a 199 U.S. gal. supplementary jettisonable tank can be carried in place of the 8x50 kg. bombs. A 20 mm cannon possibly may be mounted to fire directly above the aircraft. Radar interception equipment installed.

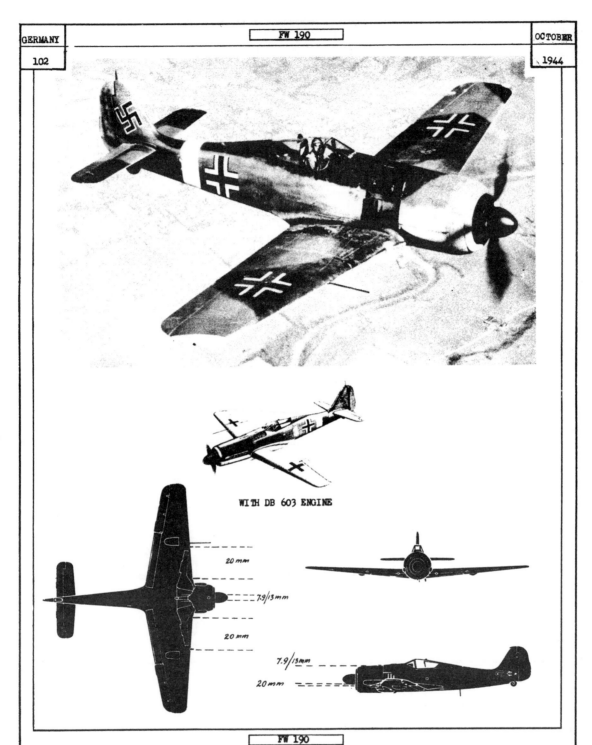

WITH DB 603 ENGINE

20 mm

7.9/13 mm

20 mm

7.9/13 mm

20 mm

FW 190

DESCRIPTION

The FW 190 is one of Germany's best fighters and is in extensive use.

It is a single-engine, low-wing, cantilever monoplane. Wing tapers moderately in plan and thickness; tips are blunt, corners rounded. Split flaps are fitted. There is a single fin and rudder. Landing gear retracts inward electrically and has an 11'-3" track; tail wheel is semi-retractable. The trimming tabs are adjustable only on the ground. A version fitted with a DB 603 engine has been reported in limited operational use. Cooling is provided with an annular radiator similar to that of the Jumo 211 engine as installed in the Ju 88 A series. Cowling is rounded into stub exhaust ports low on either side.

FW 190

SINGLE ENGINE FIGHTER

Mfr. **FOCKE-WULF**   Crew **ONE**

Duty **FIGHTING, GROUND ATTACK**

PERFORMANCE

Max. emergency speeds __330__ m. p. h. @ S. L.; __385__ m. p. h. @ __19,000__ ft. alt.; __365__ m. p. h. @ __30,000__ ft. alt.

Max. continuous speeds ___ m. p. h. @ S. L.; ___ m. p. h. @ ___ ft. alt.; ___ m. p. h. @ ___ ft. alt.

Cruising speeds: Normal __330__ m. p. h.; economical __220__ m. p. h.; ___ each at __18,000__ ft. altitude.

Climb: To __18,000__ ft. alt. in __6.5__ min.; rate ___ ft./min. at ___ ft. altitude.

Service ceilings: Normal load __36,000__ ft.; max. bomb/fuel load __28,500__ ft.; min. fuel/no bombs __38,000__ ft.

Fuel: { U. S. gal.: Normal __162__ ; max. __374__   Take-off, in calm air ___ ft.

{ Imp. gal.: Normal __115__ ; max. __310__   Take-off, over 50 ft. obstacle __1,800__ ft.

RANGES

Speeds	With Normal Fuel/Bomb Load __162__ U. S. gal. and __-__ lb. bombs	With Max. Bomb Load and __-__ U. S. gal.	With Max. Fuel Load and __-__ lb. Bombs
Economical cruising speed	@ 220 mph - 525 miles	___ miles	@ 220 mph-1,250 miles
Normal cruising speed	@ 330 mph - 445 miles	___ miles	@ 310 mph- 705 miles
Maximum continuous speed	___ miles	___ miles	___ miles
* Typical tactical speeds	___ miles	___ miles	___ miles

*Ref.: p. 4. Para. 2.

POWER PLANT

No. engines __1__ , rated 1,755 / __1,530__ hp., each at 3,250 / __20,000__ ft. alt., with 2,700 / __2,700__ r. p. m. and 41.0 / __41.0__ in. Hg.

Description __BMW 801D, 14-cylinder, twin-row, air-cooled (fan assisted) radial.__

Specifications		Supercharger	Propeller	Fuel
Bore __6.14__ in.	Dry Wgt. __2960__ lbs.	No. Speeds __2__	Mfr. __V.D.M.__	Rating __C-3, 100__ octane
Stroke __6.14__ in.	Red. Gear __541__	No. Stages ___	No. Blades __3__	Inlet System:
Displ. __2550__ cu. in.	Eng. Diam. __52__ in.	Ratios __5.31__ ; __8.32__	Diam. __10__ ft., __10__ in.	__Direct__
Comp. Ratio __7 : 1__	Eng. Length ___ in.	Impeller Diam. __13.25__ in.	Pitch Control ___	__injection__

ARMAMENT

(F—fixed. M—free.)

For'd fuselage __2x7.9/13mm (F)__

For'd wings __2/4x20mm (F)__

Through hub ___

Dorsal ___

Lateral ___

Ventral ___

Tail ___

BOMB/FREIGHT LOAD

(See Bomber Version)

Normal load ___ kg., ___ lb.

Max. load ___ kg., ___ lb.

Typical stowage __2 x 21cm rockets__

___

Alternate stowage ___

___

___

Freight ___ lb.

Troops ___

ARMOR

Frontal ___

Windshield __1 3/4" b.p. glass__

Pilot's seat __Head, shoulders, 13mm; back, 6-8mm__

Dorsal ___

Lateral ___

Ventral ___

Bulkhead ___

Engine __Cowling, 3 & 5 mm__

SPECIFICATIONS

Materials __Metal, stressed skin. A-4/U-8 sub-type has reinforced wing and fuselage.__

Span __34'-6"__   Length __29'-5"__   Height __11'-6"__   Gross wing area __197 sq. ft.__   Tail span ___

Weights: Landing __7,500__ lb.; normal load __8,600__ lb.; max. load __10,350__ lb.

ADDITIONAL TECHNICAL DATA

A-1 sub-type armed with 4x7.9 + 2x20mm MG FF: A-2, A-3, A-4 with 2x7.9 + 2xMG 151/20mm; A-5, G-3 with 2xMG 151/20mm; A-8/R-6 with 4xMG 151/20mm, 2xMG 131/13mm. Master control for boost, mixture, ignition, propeller pitch and throttle. Exhausts in three groups of four (two at sides and one beneath engine). Sub-type "B" identified, airframe differing in detail only. F-3 sub-type has lower part of cowling, wheel spats and underside of fuselage of 6 mm plate. A FW 190 version is known to be equipped with a DB 603, 12-cylinder, liquid-cooled, inverted "V" engine. Both GM-1 and methanol power-boosting installations are reported, the latter using manifold pressure of 47.68" Hg. for a period of ten minutes.

16—38265-1

HE 219

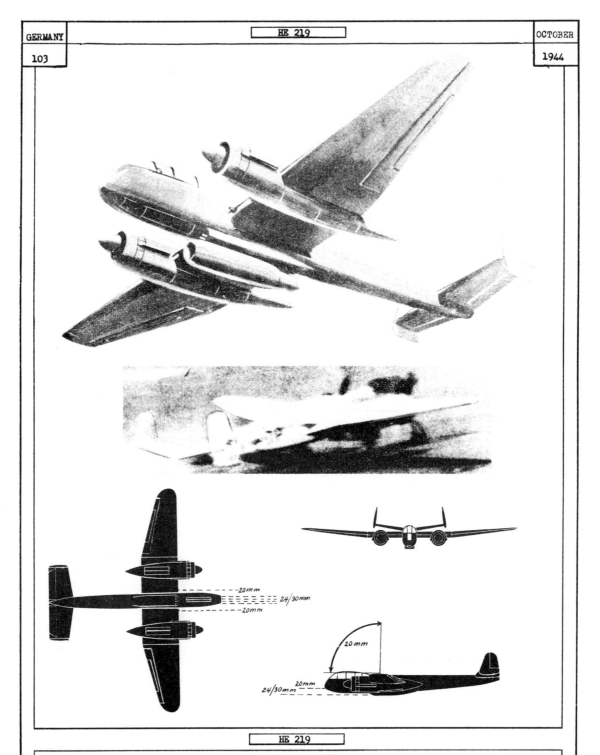

HE 219

DESCRIPTION

The He 219 is one of the newer types of German long-range fighters, used principally at night. It is a twin-engine, mid-wing monoplane. Wing center section and entire leading edge are straight; trailing edge curves slightly to rounded tips. Fuselage is long and slim with nose projecting forward of engines. Long chord engine nacelles extend beyond trailing edge. There are twin fins and rudders. The tricycle landing gear is fully retractable and consists of dual main wheels.

TWIN-ENGINE, LONG-RANGE FIGHTER

Mfr. HEINKEL   Crew PRESUMED - TWO

Duty FIGHTING, POSSIBLY DIVE BOMBING

PERFORMANCE (See additional technical data)

Max. emergency speeds (est) 325 m. p. h. @ S. L.; (est) 400 m. p. h. @ 22,000 ft. alt.; (est) 378 m. p. h. @ 14,000 ft. alt.
Max. continuous speeds _____ m. p. h. @ S. L.; _____ m. p. h. @ _____ ft. alt.; _____ m. p. h. @ _____ ft. alt.
Cruising speeds: Normal _____ m. p. h.; economical _____ m. p. h.; ___ each at _____ ft. altitude.
Climb: To _____ ft. alt. in _____ min.; rate _____ ft./min. at _____ ft. altitude.
Service ceilings: Normal load 32,900 ft.; max. bomb/fuel load 1,326 ft.; min. fuel/no bombs _____ ft.
Fuel: U. S. gal.: Normal 1,087 ; max. 1,100 Take-off, in calm air _____ ft.
Imp. gal.: Normal 902 ; max. _____ Take-off, over 50 ft. obstacle _____ ft.

RANGES

Speeds	With Normal Fuel/Bomb Load _____ U. S. gal. and _____ lb. bombs	With Max. Bomb Load and _____ U. S. gal.	With Max. Fuel Load and _____ lb. Bombs	
Economical cruising speed	_____ miles	_____ miles		_____ miles
Normal cruising speed	_____ miles	_____ miles	1545	_____ miles
Maximum continuous speed	_____ miles	_____ miles		_____ miles
*Typical tactical speeds	_____ miles	_____ miles		_____ miles

*Ref.: p. 4. Para. 2.

POWER PLANT (See additional technical data)

No. engines 2 , rated 1,800 / 1,680 hp., each at S.L. / 18,000 ft. alt., with 2,700 / 2,700 r. p. m. and 41 / 41 in. Hg.

Description DB 603, 12-cylinder, liquid-cooled, inverted "V"

Specifications	Supercharger	Propeller	Fuel
Bore 6.38 in. Dry Wgt. 2,120 lbs.	No. Speeds 1	Mfr. V.D.M.	Rating 100 octane
Stroke 7.09 in. Red. Gear .5175; .475	No. Stages	No. Blades 3	Inlet System: Direct
Displ. 2,720 cu. in. Eng. Diam. 30 in.	Ratios 9.22	Diam. 11 ft., 3 in.	injection
Comp. Ratio 7.1 Eng. Length 101 in.	Impeller Diam. 11.61 in.	Pitch Control	

ARMAMENT

(F—fixed. M—free.)

For'd fuselage . . . . . _____
For'd wings 2x20mm (F)
_____
Through hub _____
Dorsal 2x20mm (M)
Lateral _____
Ventral 4x24/30mm (F)*
Tail _____

BOMB/FREIGHT LOAD

Normal load _____ kg., _____ lb.
Max. load _____ kg., _____ lb.
Typical stowage _____
_____
_____
Alternate stowage _____
_____
Freight _____ lb.
Troops _____

ARMOR

Frontal _____
Windshield _____
Pilot's seat 15mm
Observer's seat, 15mm
Dorsal _____
Lateral _____
Ventral _____
Bulkhead _____
Engine _____

SPECIFICATIONS

Materials All metal

Span 60'-6" Length 48'-8" Height (est) 12' Gross wing area 480/500 sq.ft Tail span _____

Weights: Landing 19,900 lb.; normal load 26,100 lb.; max. load _____ lb.

ADDITIONAL TECHNICAL DATA

A turbo-jet unit is fitted optionally under the ventral bola, giving the aircraft an estimated top speed of 450 mph when in operation. It is 20' long, diameter 3'. Fuel tankage is increased to 1326 U.S. gals. when it is used. Reported that 2x20 mm are placed in a mid-dorsal position to fire both forward and at angles approaching the vertical. It is said a rocket projector tube can be mounted under each wing outboard of the nacelles. GM-1 power-boosting equipment may be fitted. Comprehensive radar installation probably is employed. A spotlight may be placed in the nose to be used when the guns are to be fired at night.
 *This new 24mm gun is reportedly a Mauser with very high muzzle velocity.

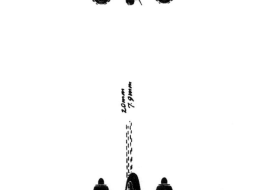

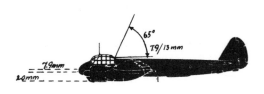

JU 88 C-5

DESCRIPTION

The Ju 88 C-5 is a fighter version of the Ju 88 bomber and is similar in appearance to the latter except for the metal-panelled nose.

It is a twin-engine, low-wing monoplane. Center section of wing is almost parallel in chord and slightly "gulled"; outer panels have "double taper". Entire trailing edge is hinged, outer portions acting as ailerons, inner sections as slotted flaps. Top and bottom of fuselage are flat; sides are curved. There is a single fin and rudder. Nose is metal-panelled to house armament and armor. Landing gear retracts rearward into nacelles, tailwheel is fixed. It may be seen with or without the ventral bola.

JU 88 C-5

TWIN-ENGINE FIGHTER

Mfr. __JUNKERS__   Crew __TWO TO THREE__

Duty __NIGHT FIGHTING, INTRUDER, GROUND ATTACK__

PERFORMANCE

Max. emergency speeds __267__ m. p. h. @ S. L.; __347__ m. p. h. @ __20,000__ ft. alt.; __304__ m. p. h. @ __25,000__ ft.alt.

Max. continuous speeds _____ m. p. h. @ S. L.; _____ m. p. h. @ _____ ft. alt.; _____ m. p. h. @ _____ ft. alt.

Cruising speeds: Normal __317__ m. p. h.; _____ economical __230__ m. p. h.; _____ each at __18,500__ ft. altitude.

Climb: To __18,500__ ft. alt. in __10.3__ min.; rate __27,800__ ft./min. at _____ ft. altitude.

Service ceilings: Normal load __30,200__ ft.; max. bomb/fuel load _____ ft.; min. fuel/no bombs __33,200__ ft.

Fuel: U. S. gal.: Normal __446__ ; max. __952__   Take-off, in calm air _____ ft.

Imp. gal.: Normal __370__ ; max. __970__   Take-off, over 50 ft. obstacle __2,310__ ft.

RANGES

Speeds	With Normal Fuel/Bomb Load __446__ U. S. gal. and __—__ lb. bombs		With Max. Bomb Load and _____ U. S. gal.	With Max. Fuel Load and __—__ lb. Bombs
Economical cruising speed	● 230 mph - 800	miles	miles	@ 243 mph-1,620 miles
Normal cruising speed	ⓑ 317 mph - 570	miles	miles	● 312 mph-1,285 miles
Maximum continuous speed		miles	miles	miles
*Typical tactical speeds		miles	miles	miles

*Ref.: p. 4. Para. 2.

POWER PLANT

No. engines __2__ , rated __1,530__ hp., each at __20,000__ ft. alt., with __2,700__ r. p. m. and __41.0__ in. Hg.

(above blanks marked: 1,755 ; 3,250 ; 2,700 ; 41.0)

Description __BMW 801D, 14-cylinder, twin-row, air-cooled, fan-assisted, radial.__

Specifications	Supercharger	Propeller	Fuel
Bore __6.14__ in. Dry Wgt. __2,960__ lbs.	No. Speeds __2__	Mfr. __V.D.M.__	Rating C-__3,100__ octane
Stroke __6.14__ in. Red. Gear __.541__	No. Stages _____	No. Blades __3__	Inlet System: _____
Displ. __2,550__ cu. in. Eng. Diam. __52__ in.	Ratios __5.31__ ; __8.32__	Diam __10__ ft., __10__ in.	__Direct injection__
Comp. Ratio __7:1__ Eng. Length _____ in.	Impeller Diam. __13.25__ in.	Pitch Control _____	

ARMAMENT

(F—fixed. M—free.)

For'd fuselage __1/3x20mm + 3x7.9 mm (F)__

For'd wings _____

Through hub _____

Dorsal __1x7.9/13mm (M) + 1 twin 20 mm (F)__

Ventral __Twin 7.9 or 1x13mm (M)__

Tail _____

BOMB/FREIGHT LOAD

Normal load _____ kg., _____ lb.

Max. load __500__ kg., __1,100__ lb.

Typical stowage _____

__10x50 kg. (110 lbs.)__

__Internal stowage.__

Alternate stowage _____

__Small number of 250 kg. (550 lbs.)__

Freight _____ lb.

Troops _____

ARMOR

Frontal __9-15 mm bulkhead.__

Windshield __1 3/4" b.p. glass__

Pilot's seat __5-9mm.__

Dorsal __5-8.5mm.__

Lateral _____

Ventral __5-8.5mm.__

Bulkhead _____

Engine _____

SPECIFICATIONS

Materials __Metal, stressed skin, flush riveting.__

Span __65'-11"__   Length __47'__   Height __16'-8"__   Gross wing area __590 sq. ft.__   Tail span _____

Weights: Landing __21,000__ lb.;   normal load __25,000__ lb.;   max. load __28,500__ lb.

ADDITIONAL TECHNICAL DATA

Engines have frontal inlet and fan-assisted cooling. Oil radiator beneath leading edge of cowling. Rear ventral guns not fitted when two "bola" guns installed. Reported C-5 has two rearward-firing guns under rear bomb bay; C-7 is said to have 2 x 7.9mm + 1 x 20mm "aft." Special night fighting equipment probably is installed. Twin dorsal 20mm believed fixed firing forward and upward at 45° angle.

20mm
20mm   7.9mm

65°
7.9mm

7.9mm
20mm

JU 88 C-6

DESCRIPTION

The Ju 88 C-6 is a fighter version of the Ju 88 bomber, similar in appearance to the A-4 sub-type except for the metal-panelled nose.

It is a twin-engine, low-wing monoplane. Center section of wing is almost parallel in chord and slightly "gulled"; outer panels have "double taper". The top and bottom of the fuselage are flat; sides are curved. There is a single fin and rudder. The nose is metal-panelled to house the armament and armor. Landing gear retracts rearward into nacelles.

JU 88C-6

TWIN ENGINE FIGHTER

Mfr. __JUNKERS__   Crew __THREE__

Duty __NIGHT FIGHTING, GROUND ATTACK__

PERFORMANCE

Max. emergency speeds __263__ m. p. h. @ S. L.; __295__ m. p. h. @ __14,000__ ft. alt.; __231__ m. p. h. @ __20,000__ ft.alt.*
Max. continuous speeds _____ m. p. h. @ S. L.; _____ m. p. h. @_____ ft. alt.; _____ m. p. h. @_____ ft. alt.
Cruising speeds: Normal __270__ m. p. h.; _____ economical __193__ m. p. h.; _____ each at __16,400__ ft. altitude.
Climb: To __16,500__ ft. alt. in_____ min.; rate_____ ft./min. at_____ ft. altitude.
Service ceilings: Normal load __24,200__ ft.; max. bomb/fuel load __23,800__ ft.; min. fuel/no bombs __31,800__ ft.
Fuel: { U. S. gal.: Normal __446__ ; max. __952__ Take-off, in calm air_____ ft.
{ Imp. gal.: Normal __370__ ; max. __790__ Take-off, over 50 ft. obstacle __2,340__ ft.

RANGES

Speeds	With Normal Fuel/Bomb Load __446__ U. S. gal. and _____ lb. bombs	With Max. Bomb Load and_____ U. S. gal.	With Max. Fuel Load and_____ lb. Bombs
Economical cruising speed	@ __193 mph - 800__ miles	miles	@ __193 mph-1,760__ miles
Normal cruising speed	@ __270 mph - 720__ miles	miles	@ __268 mph-1,710__ miles
Maximum continuous speed	miles	miles	miles
*Typical tactical speeds	__460__ miles	miles	__1,100__ miles

*Ref.: p. 4. Para. 2.

POWER PLANT

	1,380	1,350	2,600	40.5
No. engines __2__ , rated	1,305 hp., each at __12,500__ ft. alt., with	2,600 r. p. m. and	40.5 in. Hg.	

Description __Jumo 211 J, 12-cylinder, 60° liquid-cooled, inverted "V"__

Specifications	Supercharger	Propeller	Fuel
Bore __5.9__ in. Dry Wgt. __1,440__ lbs.	No. Speeds __2__	Mfr. __V.D.M., Junkers__ Rating __B-4, 87__ octane	
Stroke __6.5__ in. Red. Gear __.545__	No. Stages_____	No. Blades __3__ Inlet System:_____	
Displ. __2,130__ cu. in. Eng. Diam. __32__ in.	Ratios __8.8 ; 12.4__	Diam. ____ ft., ____ in. __Direct injection__	
Comp. Ratio __6 : 84__ Eng. Length __69__ in.	Impeller Diam. __8.91__ in.	Pitch Control_____	

ARMAMENT

(F—fixed. M—free.)

For'd fuselage __1/3x20mm +__
__3x7.9mm (F)__
For'd wings_____
Through hub_____
Dorsal __2x7.9mm(M) + 1x__
__twin 20mm (M)__
Ventral __Twin 7.9mm(M)Alternate__
Tail __for 2 bola guns.__

BOMB/FREIGHT LOAD

Normal load_____ kg., _____ lb.
Max. load __500__ kg., __1,100__ lb.
Typical stowage_____
__Internal stowage__
__10x50 kg. (110 lb.)__
Alternate stowage_____
Freight_____ lb.
Troops_____

ARMOR

Frontal __9mm slats__
Windshield __1 3/4" b.p. glass__
Pilot's seat __Seat, 4mm__
__Back, 9mm__
Dorsal __5-8.5mm__
Lateral_____
Ventral __5-8.5mm__
Bulkhead __15mm circular(frontal)__
Engine_____

SPECIFICATIONS

Materials __Metal, stressed skin, flush riveting__

Span __65'-11"__ Length __47'__ Height __16'-7"__ Gross wing area __590 sq. ft.__ Tail span_____

Weights: Landing __20,000__ lb.; normal load __24,000__ lb.; max. load __27,500__ lb.

ADDITIONAL TECHNICAL DATA

C-2 has Jumo 211F engine; C-4 has auxiliary reconnaissance equipment. 13mm guns may replace the 7.9mm
guns. Engine fitted with induction air cooler. Nacelles of circular section carrying frontal radiators with adjustable gills. Hot air de-icing for leading edge of wing; Goodrich pulsating system
on stabilizer leading edge. Propeller de-icing is provided. Elaborate radio and radar installations.
A Ju 88C-6 has been found with BMW 801 D-2 engines, as in the C-5 version and performance would be
increased accordingly. Four cement blocks are carried in the rear fuselage as ballast. 20mm cannon
have 120 rpg., forward 7.9 mm 1,000 rpg. and dorsal 7.9mm 500 rpg. Latest development is believed to
be twin dorsal 20 mm cannon fixed firing forward at ρ 45° angle.

ME 109E

DESCRIPTION

The Me 109E was developed from the original Me 109 which appeared in 1936 - 1937. Up to the end of 1940, it was the standard single-seat fighter of the G.A.F. It has been superseded since as a first-line fighter in the Me 109 series by, in turn, the F and the G sub-types. Indications are that a limited number of Me 109 E's may still be employed in ground attack and fighter-bomber operations, but their main role today is that of advanced trainers.

It is a single-engine, low-wing monoplane. Wing tapers to square tips with rounded corners. Automatic slots and slotted flaps are fitted. The strut-braced stabilizer is adjustable; rudder and elevator are balanced. Landing gear retracts outward hydraulically. The tailwheel is fixed.

ME 109 E

SINGLE-ENGINE FIGHTER/BOMBER

Mfr. MESSERSCHMITT   Crew   ONE

Duty GROUND-ATTACK, BOMBING, FIGHTING IN EMERGENCY, ADVANCED TRAINING

PERFORMANCE

Max. emergency speeds 300 m. p. h. @ S. L.; 355 m. p. h. @ 18,000 ft. alt.; 320 m. p. h. @ 30,000 ft. alt.
Max. continuous speeds _____ m. p. h. @ S. L.; _____ m. p. h. @ _____ ft. alt.; _____ m. p. h. @ _____ ft. alt.
Cruising speeds: Normal 300 m. p. h.; economical 200 m. p. h.; _____ each at 16,500 ft. altitude.
Climb: To 16,500 ft. alt. in 6.2 min.; rate _____ ft./min. at _____ ft. altitude.
Service ceilings: Normal load 35,000 ft.; max. bomb/fuel load 33,000 ft.; min. fuel/no bombs 36,500 ft.
Fuel: { U. S. gal.: Normal 106 ; max. 186 Take-off, in calm air _____ ft.
{ Imp. gal.: Normal 88 ; max. 154 Take-off, over 50 ft. obstacle 1,260 ft.

RANGES

Speeds	With Normal Fuel/Bomb Load 106 U.S. gal. and — lb. bombs		With Max. Bomb Load and 106 U.S. gal.		With Max. Fuel Load and — lb. Bombs	
Economical cruising speed	ⓔ 200 mph – 655	miles	ⓔ 200 mph-550	miles	ⓔ 200 mph-1,050	miles
Normal cruising speed	ⓔ 300 mph - 450	miles	ⓔ 285 mph-420	miles	ⓔ 285 mph-800	miles
Maximum continuous speed		miles		miles		miles
*Typical tactical speeds	315	miles	290	miles	633	miles

*Ref.: p. 4. Para. 2.

POWER PLANT

	1,175	6,000	2,400	40.5
No. engines 1 , rated 1,070 hp., each at 12,250 ft. alt., with 2,400 r. p. m. and 40.5 in. Hg.

Description DB 601A, 12-cylinder, liquid-cooled, inverted "V"

Specifications	Supercharger	Propeller	Fuel
Bore 5.91 in. Dry Wgt. 1,400 lbs.	No. Speeds 1	Mfr. V.D.M.	Rating 87 octane
Stroke 6.30 in. Red. Gear .6425	No. Stages _____	No. Blades 3	Inlet System:
Displ. 2,070 cu. in. Eng. Diam. 30 in.	Ratios 10.39	Diam 10 ft. 2 in.	Direct injection
Comp. Ratio 6.9:1 Eng. Length 68.5 in.	Impeller Diam. 10.24 in.	Pitch Control _____	

ARMAMENT

(F—fixed. M—free.)

For'd fuselage 2x7.9mm (F)
1,000 rpg.
For'd wings 2x20mm (F)
60 rpg.
Through hub _____
Dorsal _____
Lateral _____
Ventral _____
Tail _____

BOMB/FREIGHT LOAD

Normal load _____ kg., _____ lb.
Max. load _____ kg., 550 lb.
Typical stowage _____
4x50 kg. (110 lb.)
Alternate stowage _____
1x250 kg (550 lb.)
92x2 kg (4.4 lb.)
Freight _____ lb.
Troops _____

ARMOR

Frontal _____
Windshield 2" bullet-proof glass
Pilot's seat Head, 10mm
Back, 4 mm
Dorsal _____
Lateral _____
Ventral _____
Bulkhead 8mm, 5' behind pilot
Engine 5mm below radiators, oil cooler, fuel pump

SPECIFICATIONS

Materials All metal, stressed skin

Span 32'-6" Length 29' Height 10'-6" Gross wing area 175 sq. ft. Tail span _____

Weights: Landing 5,000 lb.; normal load 5,850 lb.; max. load 6,500 lb.

ADDITIONAL TECHNICAL DATA

Coolant radiators under wings. Oil radiator under rear of engine. Intake blower on left side of engine. Some ME 109 E's have a DB 601 N engine. Bomb carrier is under fuselage only. When carrying bomb load, no jettisonable fuel tank can be slung. GM-1 power-boosting system may be installed.

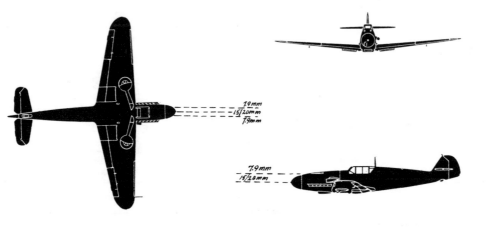

ME 109 F-4

DESCRIPTION

The Me 109 F-4 is one of Germany's older single-engine fighters. The tropical version, fitted with an air cleaner, was in extensive use in North Africa. The Me 109F series has been replaced for the most part by the later G series.

It is a single-engine, low-wing monoplane. Many of its structural components are similar to those of the Me 109E. Wings are of different section than those of the Me 109E and taper to rounded tips. Automatic slots and slotted flaps are fitted. Inclosed cockpit, with a jettisonable cover, is placed over the wing. Rudder and elevators are balanced. Landing gear retracts outward into wings; tailwheel also retracts.

ME 109 F-4

SINGLE-ENGINE FIGHTER

Mfr. MESSERSCHMITT   Crew ONE

Duty FIGHTING, GROUND ATTACK, RECONNAISSANCE

PERFORMANCE

Max. emergency speeds 315 m. p. h. @ S. L.; 395 m. p. h. @ 22,000 ft. alt.; 375 m. p. h. @ 30,000 ft.alt.

Max. continuous speeds ___ m. p. h. @ S. L.; ___ m. p. h. @ ___ ft. alt.; ___ m. p. h. @ ___ ft. alt.

Cruising speeds: Normal 320 m. p. h.; economical 200 m. p. h.; ___ each at 17,000 ft. altitude.

Climb: To 17,000 ft. alt. in 5.75 min.; rate ___ ft./min. at ___ ft. altitude.

Service ceilings: Normal load 36,500 ft.; max. bomb/fuel load 34,000 ft.; min. fuel/no bombs 38,000 ft.

Fuel: { U. S. gal.: Normal 106 ; max. 186 Take-off, in calm air ___ ft.

{ Imp. gal.: Normal 88 ; max. 154 Take-off, over 50 ft. obstacle 1575 ft.

RANGES

Speeds	With Normal Fuel/Bomb Load 106 U. S. gal. and ___ lb. bombs	With Max. Bomb Load and ___ U. S. gal.	With Max. Fuel Load and ___ lb. Bombs
Economical cruising speed	@ 200 mph – 650 miles	___ miles	@ 200 mph–1,060 miles
Normal cruising speed	@ 320 mph – 470 miles	___ miles	@ 305 mph– 830 miles
Maximum continuous speed	. ___ miles	___ miles	___ miles
*Typical tactical speeds	330 miles	315 miles	670 miles

*Ref.: p. 4. Para. 2.

POWER PLANT

No. engines 1 , rated 1,220 hp., each at 15,000 ft. alt., with 2,500 r. p. m. and 37.57 in. Hg.

1,395   S.L.   2,700   41.04

Description DB 601E, 12-cylinder, liquid-cooled, inverted "V"

Specifications	Supercharger	Propeller	Fuel
Bore 5.91 in. Dry Wgt. 1,500 lbs.	No. Speeds 1	Mfr. V.D.M.	Rating 87 octane
Stroke 6.30 in. Red. Gear .595	No. Stages ___	No. Blades 3	Inlet System: Direct
Displ. 2,070 cu. in. Eng. Diam. 29 in.	Ratios 10.07	Diam. 9 ft., 8 in.	injection
Comp. Ratio 7 1 Eng. Length 68 in.	Impeller Diam. 10.25 in.	Pitch Control ___	

ARMAMENT

(F—fixed. M—free.)

For'd fuselage 2x7.9mm (F) 500 rpg

For'd wings occ. 2x20mm

Through hub 1x15/20mm (F)

Dorsal 200 rds

Lateral ___

Ventral ___

Tail ___

BOMB/FREIGHT LOAD

See Bomber Version

Normal load ___ kg., ___ lb.

Max. load ___ kg., ___ lb.

Typical stowage ___

Possibly 2x21 cm. rockets under wing

Alternate stowage ___

Freight ___ lb.

Troops ___

ARMOR

Frontal ___

Windshield 2-1/4" bulletproof glass

Pilot's seat Head, 8 mm

Back, 5-8mm

Dorsal ___

Lateral ___

Ventral ___

Bulkhead Laminated 20mm dural behind fuel tank.

Engine ___

SPECIFICATIONS

Materials Metal, stressed skin, flush riveting

Span 32'-8"   Length 29'-11"   Height 10'-6"   Gross wing area 172 sq. ft.   Tail span ___

Weights: Landing 5,700 lb.; normal load 6,420 lb.; max. load 6,980 lb.

ADDITIONAL TECHNICAL DATA

Coolant radiators, incorporating boundary layer by-pass, under wings. Oil radiator under rear of engine. Intake blower on left side of engine. GM-1 power-boosting equipment can be fitted for short emergency acceleration at altitude. Fuel tanks without self-sealing rubber covering are sometimes fitted. When 2x20 mm are fitted under wings, maximum speeds are reduced by about 25 mph, service ceilings by about 1,000 ft and climb by 8%.

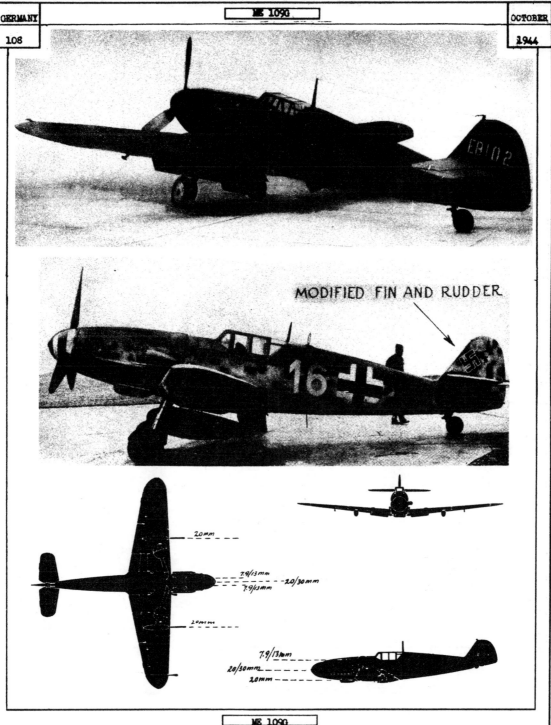

MODIFIED FIN AND RUDDER

ME 109G

DESCRIPTION

The Me 109G appeared in service in September, 1942 and is the latest and one of the best German single-seat fighters.

It is a single-engine, low-wing monoplane, developed from and almost identical with the Me 109F. Wings taper to rounded tips. A prominent fairing is fitted under each wing to house a wing gun. Automatic slots and slotted flaps are fitted. Inclosed cockpit, with a jettisonable cover, is placed over the wing. Rudder and elevators are balanced. Landing gear retracts outward into wings; tailwheel also retracts. Some newer G-6 models have new tail constructed of plywood; rudder has no projecting horn, the hinge line being straight, with metal balance weight near top. A section of the fin is cut out to allow weight to swing. Tail unit of these versions has more rounded top; fin and rudder has much cleaner and taller appearance.

ME 109 G

SINGLE-ENGINE FIGHTER

Mfr. MESSERSCHMITT   Crew ONE

Duty FIGHTING, GROUND ATTACK, RECONNAISSANCE

PERFORMANCE

Max. emergency speeds 330 m. p. h. @ S. L.; 400 m. p. h. @ 22,000 ft. alt.; 380 m. p. h. @ 30,000 ft. alt.

Max. continuous speeds _____ m. p. h. @ S. L.; _____ m. p. h. @ _____ ft. alt.; _____ m. p. h. @ _____ ft. alt.

Cruising speeds: Normal 330 m. p. h.; economical 200 m. p. h.; each at 19,000 ft. altitude.

Climb: To 19,000 ft. alt. in 6 min.; rate _____ ft./min. at _____ ft. altitude.

Service ceilings: Normal load 38,500 ft.; max. bomb/fuel load 35,500 ft.; min. fuel/no bombs 39,750 ft.

Fuel: { U. S. gal.: Normal 106 ; max. 186   Take-off, in calm air _____ ft.
{ Imp. gal.: Normal 88 ; max. 154   Take-off, over 50 ft. obstacle 1500 ft.

RANGES

Speeds	With Normal Fuel/Bomb Load 106 U. S. gal. and _____ lb. bombs	With Max. Bomb Load and _____ U. S. gal.	With Max. Fuel Load and _____ lb. Bombs
Economical cruising speed	● 200 mph – 615 miles	_____ miles	● 200 mph–1045 miles
Normal cruising speed	● 330 mph – 450 miles	_____ miles	● 310 mph– 795 miles
Maximum continuous speed	_____ miles	_____ miles	_____ miles
* Typical tactical speeds	315 miles	_____ miles	630 miles

*Ref.: p. 4. Para. 2.

POWER PLANT

	1,460	S.L.	2,800	41.04

No. engines 1 , rated 1,340 hp., each at 18,700 ft. alt., with 2,800 r. p. m. and 41.04 in. Hg.

Description DB 605 A/1, 12-cylinder, liquid-cooled, inverted "V".

Specifications	Supercharger	Propeller	Fuel
Bore 6.06 in. Dry Wgt. 1,550 lbs.	No. Speeds 1	Mfr. V.D.M.	Rating 87/100 octane
Stroke 6.3 in. Red. Gear .5925	No. Stages _____	No. Blades 3	Inlet System: Direct
Displ. 2,185 cu. in. Eng. Diam. 29 in.	Ratios 10.07	Diam. 9 ft. 10 in.	injection
Comp. Ratio 7 : 77 Eng. Length 68 in.	Impeller Diam. 10.48 in. 12.2	Pitch Control _____	

ARMAMENT

(F—fixed. M—free.)

For'd fuselage 2x7.9/13mm (F)
   500 rpg.
For'd wings 2x20mm (F)
   200 rpg
Through hub 1x20/30mm (F)
Dorsal _____
Lateral _____
Ventral _____
Tail _____

BOMB/FREIGHT LOAD

See Bomber Version

Normal load _____ kg., _____ lb.
Max. load _____ kg., _____ lb.
Typical stowage
   2x21cm. rockets
   under wing
Alternate stowage _____
_____
_____
Freight _____ lb.
Troops _____

ARMOR

Frontal _____
Windshield 2-1/2" bulletproof glass
Pilot's seat Head, 8mm
   Back 5-10mm
Dorsal (rear) 2 5/8" b.p.glass & 5-10 mm plate.
Ventral Radiators, 5mm
Bulkhead Laminated 20 mm dural behind fuel tank
Engine _____

SPECIFICATIONS

Materials Metal, stressed skin. Sometimes wooden tail unit.

Span 32'-8"   Length 29'-11"   Height 10'-6"   Gross wing area 172 sq. ft.   Tail span _____

Weights: Landing 5,900 lb.; normal load 6,820 lb.; max. load 7,230 lb.

ADDITIONAL TECHNICAL DATA

Wing 20mm are fitted in fairings under wing. GM-1 equipment can be fitted for short emergency acceleration at altitude. Sub-types G-1, G-3, and G-5 have pressurizing equipment for sustained operation at high altitudes. Port wing carries oxygen bottles. When wing guns are fitted, max. speeds are reduced by about 25 mph, service ceilings by about 1,000 feet and climb by 8%. G-8 and 14 sub-types use C-3, 100 octane fuel and methanol injections, "MW-50", is used with 49" Hg. manifold pressure and larger supercharger enabling an extra speed of from about 37-43 mph to be attained. When using the "MW-50", 49" Hg. and 2,800 rpm, estimated power output is 1,700 hp. Two 12.5 cm cameras are sometimes installed in rear fuselage. Late sub-types incorporate greater use of wood and plywood as substitutes for metal. Me 109 T is used for deck landing. Ultra-violet lighting of cockpit is used. Oxygen flow is automatically controlled by a barometric capsule.

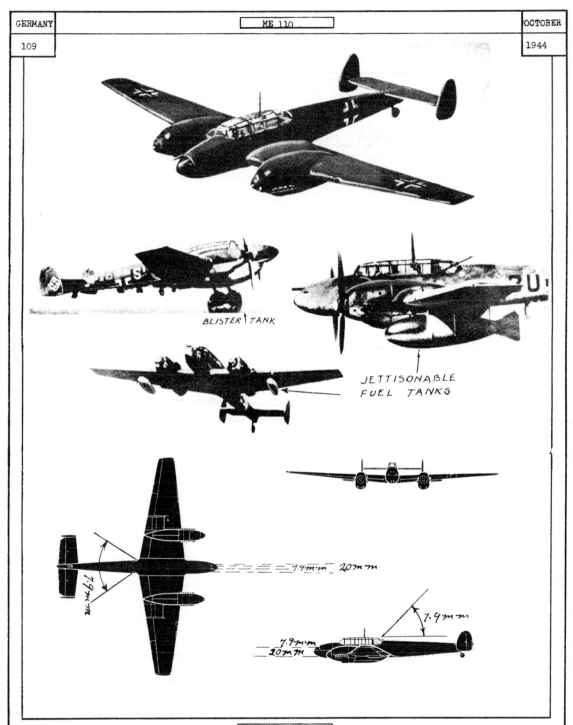

BLISTER TANK

JETTISONABLE
FUEL TANKS

7.9mm   20mm

7.9mm
20mm

7.9mm

ME 110

DESCRIPTION

The Me 110 fitted with DB 601 engines was in 1939 Germany's standard long range, twin-engined fighter. Although now superseded by the Me 410 and the Me 110G with DB 605 engines, it is still extensively employed as a rocket-firing defense fighter against day bombers, as a night-fighter and as a fast glider tug.

It is a twin-engine, low-wing monoplane. The narrow wings taper to square tips, with slightly rounded corners. There are slots, slotted flaps, and "drooping" ailerons. Fuselage is of slim, oval section. The cockpit inclosure is long and transparent. Landing gear retracts hydraulically rearward into nacelles; tailwheel is fixed.

ME 110

TWIN-ENGINE FIGHTER

Mfr. __MESSERSCHMITT__   Crew __TWO__

Duty __FIGHTING, GROUND ATTACK, RECONNAISSANCE, GLIDER TUG__

PERFORMANCE

Max. emergency speeds __300__ m. p. h. @ S. L.; __360__ m. p. h. @ __20,000__ ft. alt.; __337__ m. p. h. @ __30,000__ ft.alt.

Max. continuous speeds_____ m. p. h. @ S. L.; _____ m. p. h. @ _____ ft. alt.; _____ m. p. h. @ _____ ft. alt.

Cruising speeds: Normal __300__ m. p. h.; ____ economical __200__ m. p. h.; ____ each at __18,000__ ft. altitude.

Climb: To __18,000__ ft. alt. in __9.5__ min.; rate _____ ft./min. at _____ ft. altitude.

Service ceilings: Normal load __34,000__ ft.; max. bomb/fuel load __28,000__ ft.; min. fuel/no bombs __36,000__ ft.

Fuel: { U. S. gal.: Normal __337__ ; max. __813__ — Take-off, in calm air _____ ft.

{ Imp. gal.: Normal __280__ ; max. __675__ — Take-off, over 50 ft. obstacle _____ ft.

RANGES

Speeds	With Normal Fuel/Bomb Load __337__ U. S. gal. and __—__ lb. bombs	With Max. Bomb Load and _____ U. S. gal.	With Max. Fuel Load and __615__ lb. Bombs
Economical cruising speed	@ 200 mph – 930 miles	_____ miles	@ 200 mph–1920 miles
Normal cruising speed	@ 300 mph – 690 miles	_____ miles	@ 270 mph–1635 miles
Maximum continuous speed	_____ miles	_____ miles	_____ miles
*Typical tactical speeds	450 miles	_____ miles	1100 miles

*Ref.: p. 4. Para. 2.

POWER PLANT

	1,395	S.L.	2,700	41.0

No. engines __2__ , rated __1,220__ hp., each at __15,000__ ft. alt., with __2,500__ r. p. m. and __37.57__ in. Hg.

Description __DB 601F, 12-cylinder, liquid-cooled, inverted "V"__

Specifications	Supercharger	Propeller	Fuel
Bore __5.91__ in. Dry Wgt. __1,500__ lbs.	No. Speeds __1__	Mfr. __V.D.M.__	Rating __87__ octane
Stroke __6.30__ in. Red. Gear __.595__	No. Stages ____	No. Blades __3__	Inlet System: __Direct__
Displ. __2,070__ cu. in. Eng. Diam. __29__ in.	Ratios __10.07__	Diam 9 ft. __10__ in.	__injection__
Comp. Ratio __7__ : __1__ Eng. Length __68__ in.	Impeller Diam. __10.25__ in.	Pitch Control __Electro-mechanical__	

ARMAMENT

(F—fixed.   M—free.)

For'd fuselage __4x7.9mm 1000 rpg.__
+ 2/4x20mm, 240 rpg (F)

For'd wings _____

Through hub _____
Dorsal 1/twinx7.9mm (M)

Lateral _____

Ventral _____

Tail _____

BOMB/FREIGHT LOAD

See bomber version

Normal load _____ kg., _____ lb.

Max. load _____ kg., _____ lb.

Typical stowage _____

Alternate stowage _____

Freight _____ lb.

Troops _____

ARMOR

Frontal __9 mm__

Windshield __2¼" b.p. glass__

Pilot's seat __Head, 11mm__
__Back, 8mm__

Dorsal _____

Lateral _____

Ventral __6mm__

Bulkhead __8mm behind radio operator__

Engine occ. 5mm behind spinner protects coolant heater tank and reduction gears.

SPECIFICATIONS

Materials __Metal, stressed skin, flush riveting.__

Span __53'-11"__   Length __40'-3"__   Height __11'-6"__   Gross wing area __415 sq. ft.__   Tail span _____

Weights: Landing __14,000__ lb.;   normal load __16,200__ lb.;   max. load __20,400__ lb.

ADDITIONAL TECHNICAL DATA

Coolant radiators under wings; oil radiator under rear of engine. 1x30 mm can be fitted as
alternative to 2x20mm. Provision is made for 268 gal. "blister" fuel tank under the fuselage;
jettisonable fuel tanks can be fitted under wings and an additional oil tank then is carried. In
reconnaissance condition 2x20mm are omitted. Recent series may have span of 55'-5".

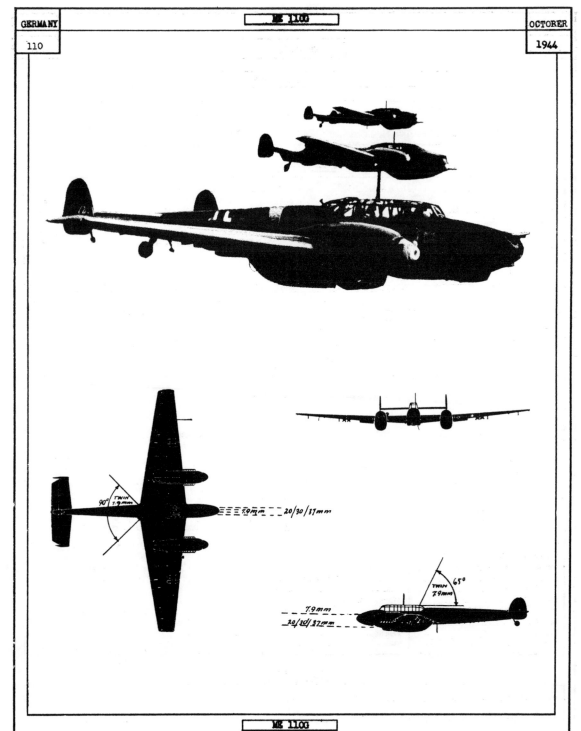

ME 110G

DESCRIPTION

The Me 110 G sub-series is identical in appearance with the Me 110 and differs only in the fitting of more powerful engines. The performance is correspondingly improved.

It is a twin-engine, low-wing monoplane. The narrow wings taper to square tips, with slightly rounded corners. There are slots, slotted flaps, and "drooping" ailerons. Fuselage is of slim, oval section. The cockpit inclosure is long and transparent. Landing gear retracts hydraulically rearward into nacelles; tailwheel is fixed.

ME 110 G

TWIN-ENGINE FIGHTER

Mfr. MESSERSCHMITT   Crew TWO

Duty FIGHTING, GROUND ATTACK, RECONNAISSANCE, GLIDER TUG.

PERFORMANCE

Max. emergency speeds __310__ m. p. h. @ S. L.; __368__ m. p. h. @ __19,000__ ft. alt.; __355__ m. p. h. @ __30,000__ ft.alt.

Max. continuous speeds ____ m. p. h. @ S. L.; ____ m. p. h. @ ____ ft. alt.; ____ m. p. h. @ ____ ft. alt.

Cruising speeds: Normal __305__ m. p. h.; economical __205__ m. p. h.; each at __18,000__ ft. altitude.

Climb: To __18,000__ ft. alt. in __7.3__ min.; rate ____ ft./min. at ____ ft. altitude.

Service ceilings: Normal load __34,800__ ft.; max. bomb/fuel load __29,000__ ft.; min. fuel/no bombs __36,800__ ft.

Fuel: { U. S. gal.: Normal __337__ ; max. __813__ Take-off, in calm air ____ ft.

{ Imp. gal.: Normal __280__ ; max. __675__ Take-off, over 50 ft. obstacle ____ ft.

RANGES

Speeds	With Normal Fuel/Bomb Load __337__ U. S. gal. and __-__ lb. bombs	With Max. Bomb Load and ____ U. S. gal.	With Max. Fuel Load and ____ lb. Bombs
Economical cruising speed	@ 205 mph – 905 miles	____ miles	@ 205 mph–1,700 miles
Normal cruising speed	@ 305 mph – 690 miles	____ miles	@ 280 mph–1,440 miles
Maximum continuous speed	____ miles	____ miles	____ miles
*Typical tactical speeds	450 miles	400 miles	940 miles

*Ref.: p. 4. Para. 2.

POWER PLANT

	1,460	S.L.	2,800	41.04

No. engines __2__ , rated __1,340__ hp., each at __18,700__ ft. alt., with __2,800__ r. p. m. and __41.04__ in. Hg.

Description DB 605B, 12-cylinder, liquid-cooled, inverted "V"

Specifications	Supercharger	Propeller	Fuel
Bore 6.06 in. Dry Wgt. 1,680 lbs.	No. Speeds 1	Mfr. V.D.M.	Rating B-4.87 octane
Stroke 6.30 in. Red. Gear .534	No. Stages	No. Blades 3	Inlet System: Direct
Displ.2,180 cu. in. Eng. Diam. 29 in.	Ratios 10.07	Diam9 ft. 10 in.	injection
Comp. Ratio 7.77 Eng. Length 68 in.	Impeller Diam. 10.48 in.	Pitch Control Electro-mechanical	

ARMAMENT

(F—fixed. M—free.)

For'd fuselage 4x7.9mm,1000rpg
+ 2/4x20mm, 350 rpg. or

For'd wings 1x37mm, 72 rds +
2x30mm, 135 rpg. (F)

Through hub ____

Dorsal 1 Twin 7.9mm (M)

Lateral ____ (400 rpg)

Ventral ____

Tail occ. 1x20mm (F) 350 rds.

BOMB/FREIGHT LOAD

See Bomber Version

Normal load ____ kg., ____ lb.

Max. load ____ kg., ____ lb.

Typical stowage ____
2x21cm rocket launchers carried under
each outboard wing section

Alternate stowage ____

Freight ____ lb.

Troops ____

ARMOR

Frontal Sides & bulkheads 8 – 10mm

Windshield 1 1/2" b.p. glass

Pilot's seat Head, 11 mm
Back, 8mm

Dorsal ____

Lateral ____

Ventral 6 mm

Bulkhead 8 mm behind radio
operator

Engine occ. 5mm behind spinner
protects coolant header tank
and reduction gears

SPECIFICATIONS

Materials Metal, stressed skin, flush riveting

Span 53'11"   Length 40'-4"   Height 11'-6"   Gross wing area 415 sq. ft.   Tail span ____

Weights: Landing 16,510 lb.;   normal load 18,000 lb.;   max. load 20,700 lb.

ADDITIONAL TECHNICAL DATA

Coolant radiators under wings. Oil radiator under rear of engine. Nose of H-2 sub-type, housing
2x30mm, is modified. G & H sub-types have been strengthened, tailwheel on latter is rectract-
able. GM-1 power-boosting apparatus with 45 min. duration is sometimes fitted. Oxygen bottles
are stowed behind cross bulkhead level with the trailing edge. Reports indicate some night fighters
are fitted with 2x20 mm cannon placed to fire forward at 45° angle. Alternate armament may be
1x30 mm + 3x7.9mm forward fuselage, 2x20mm ventral, possibly 2x20mm in ventral bola, twin 7.9mm
dorsal and above angular 20mm cannon. G-2 is fighter, G-3 reconnaissance, G-4 night fighter.
Maximum permissible diving speed 435 mph.

16—35255-1

ME 163

DESCRIPTION

The Me 163 is a liquid-rocket-propelled interceptor fighter.

It is a single-seat, mid-wing monoplane, reportedly of mixed metal and wood construction. In plan view it resembles somewhat an arrow head. The G.A.F. have nicknamed it the "Moth". Wings are sharply swept-back, tips rounded. Fuselage is very short, being "tear-drop" in shape and unusually deep in relation to its length. There is a single fin and rudder; stabilizer and elevators are not employed.

ME 163

LIQUID-ROCKET-PROPELLED INTERCEPTOR FIGHTER.

Mfr. MESSERSCHMITT.   Crew   ONE

Duty FIGHTING.

PERFORMANCE

Max. emergency speeds _____ m. p. h. @ S. L.; _500/600_ m. p. h. @ _____ ft. alt.; _____ m. p. h. @ _____ ft.alt.
Max. continuous speeds _____ m. p. h. @ S. L.; _____ m. p. h. @ _____ ft. alt.; _____ m. p. h. @ _____ ft. alt.
Cruising speeds: Normal _____ m. p. h.; __ economical _____ m. p. h.; __ each at _____ _____ ft. altitude.
Climb: To _15,000_ ft. alt. in _3_ min.; rate _10,000_ ft./min. at _40,000_ ft. altitude.
Service ceilings: Normal load _____ ft.; max. bomb/fuel load _____ ft.; min. fuel/no bombs _____ ft.
Fuel: { U. S. gal.: Normal (est) 398 ; max. _____ Take-off, in calm air _____ ft.
       { Imp. gal.: Normal (est) 330 ; max. _____ Take-off, over 50 ft. obstacle 3600 ft.

RANGES

Speeds	With Normal Fuel/Bomb Load U. S. gal. and _____ lb. bombs		With Max. Bomb Load and _____ U. S. gal.	With Max. Fuel Load and _____ lb. Bombs
Economical cruising speed	_____ miles		_____ miles	_____ miles
Normal cruising speed	_____ miles		_____ miles	_____ miles
Maximum continuous speed	_____ miles		_____ miles	_____ miles
*Typical tactical speeds	_____ miles		_____ miles	_____ miles

*Ref.: p. 4. Para. 2.

POWER PLANT

No. engines __1__ , rated _____ hp., each at _____ ft. alt., with _____ r. p. m. and _____ in. Hg.

Description 1 Liquid rocket propulsion unit, designed by Walter of Kiel.

Specifications	Supercharger	Propeller	Fuel
Bore _____ in. Dry Wgt. _____ lbs.	No. Speeds _____	Mfr. _____	Rating _____ octane
Stroke _____ in. Red. Gear ____ : ____	No. Stages _____	No. Blades _____	Inlet System: _____
Displ. _____ cu. in. Eng. Diam. _____ in.	Ratios _____	Diam. __ ft., __ in.	
Comp. Ratio __ : _____ Eng. Length _____ in.	Impeller Diam. _____ in.	Pitch Control _____	

ARMAMENT

(F—fixed.   M—free.)
(Probable)
For'd fuselage 2 x 20/30mm (F)

For'd wings 2 x 20/30mm (F)

Through hub _____
Dorsal _____
Lateral _____
Ventral _____
Tail _____

BOMB/FREIGHT LOAD

Normal load _____ kg., _____ lb.
Max. load _____ kg., _____ lb.
Typical stowage _____
_____
_____
Alternate stowage _____
_____
Freight _____ lb.
Troops _____

ARMOR

Frontal _____
Windshield _____
Pilot's seat _____

Dorsal _____
Lateral _____
Ventral _____
Bulkhead _____
Engine _____

SPECIFICATIONS

Materials Metal, wood.

Span (est) 31'   Length (est) 23'   Height _____ Gross wing area _____ Tail span _____

Weights: Landing _____ lb.; normal load _____ lb.; max. load _____ lb.

ADDITIONAL TECHNICAL DATA

Endurance of rocket unit at full power - 7 to 10 min. Time in the air may be increased to 40 minutes by alternating powered and gliding flight. Two small wheels are used for take-off and are jettisoned thereafter. Aircraft lands on skid which probably incorporates braking device.

ME 262

DESCRIPTION

The Me 262 is a "turbine-type" jet-propelled aircraft.
It is a single-seat, all-metal, twin-unit, low-wing monoplane. Wings are tapered, tips square. Nose is long and pointed. Propulsion units are slung underneath wings. Tricycle landing gear is retractable.

ME 262

JET-PROPELLED TURBINE TYPE FIGHTER

Mfr. **MESSERSCHMITT** _____ Crew **ONE** _____

Duty **FIGHTING, POSSIBLY GROUND ATTACK, RECONNAISSANCE** _____

PERFORMANCE

Max. emergency speeds _____ m. p. h. @ S. L.; **(est) 550** m. p. h. @ _____ ft. alt.; _____ m. p. h. @ _____ ft.alt.
Max. continuous speeds _____ m. p. h. @ S. L.; _____ m. p. h. @ _____ ft. alt.; _____ m. p. h. @ _____ ft. alt.
Cruising speeds: Normal _____ m. p. h.; economical _____ m. p. h.; _____ each at _____ ft. altitude.
Climb: To _____ ft. alt. in _____ min.; rate _____ ft./min. at _____ ft. altitude.
Service ceilings: Normal load _____ ft.; max. bomb/fuel load _____ ft.; min. fuel/no bombs _____ ft.
Fuel: U. S. gal.: Normal _____ ; max. _____ Take-off, in calm air _____ ft.
Imp. gal.: Normal _____ ; max. _____ Take-off, over 50 ft. obstacle _____ ft.

RANGES

Speeds	With Normal Fuel/Bomb Load _____ U. S. gal. and _____ lb. bombs	With Max. Bomb Load and _____ U. S. gal.	With Max. Fuel Load and _____ lb. Bombs
Economical cruising speed	_____ miles	_____ miles	_____ miles
Normal cruising speed	_____ miles	_____ miles	_____ miles
Maximum continuous speed	_____ miles	_____ miles	_____ miles
*Typical tactical speeds	_____ miles	_____ miles	_____ miles

*Ref.: p. 4. Para. 2.

POWER PLANT

No. engines **2**, rated _____ hp., each at _____ ft. alt., with _____ r. p. m. and _____ in. Hg.

Description **Two turbine-type jet propulsion units** _____

Specifications	Supercharger	Propeller	Fuel
Bore _____ in. Dry Wgt. _____ lbs.	No. Speeds _____	Mfr. _____	Rating _____ octane
Stroke _____ in. Red. Gear _____ : _____	No. Stages _____	No. Blades _____	Inlet System: _____
Displ. _____ cu. in. Eng. Diam. _____ in.	Ratios _____	Diam. _____ ft., _____ in.	
Comp. Ratio _____ : _____ Eng. Length _____ in.	Impeller Diam. _____ in.	Pitch Control _____	

ARMAMENT

(F—fixed. M—free.)

For'd fuselage **30mm, number unknown. Poss.20mm carried** For'd wings **also.**
_____
Through hub _____
Dorsal _____
Lateral _____
Ventral _____
Tail _____

BOMB/FREIGHT LOAD

Normal load _____ kg., _____ lb.
Max. load _____ kg., _____ lb.
Typical stowage _____
Alternate stowage _____
Freight _____ lb.
Troops _____

ARMOR

Frontal _____
Windshield _____
Pilot's seat _____
Dorsal _____
Lateral _____
Ventral _____
Bulkhead _____
Engine _____

SPECIFICATIONS

Materials _____

Span **(est) 41'** Length **(est) 35'-5"** Height _____ Gross wing area **(est) 226 sq.ft** Tail span _____

Weights: Landing _____ lb.; normal load _____ lb.; max. load _____ lb.

ADDITIONAL TECHNICAL DATA

590 TOPSPEED

HE 280

DESCRIPTION

The He 280 is a "turbine-type", jet-propelled aircraft.
It is a single-seat, twin-unit, all-metal, low-wing monoplane. Fuselage is slim and nose pointed. Wing leading edge is straight, trailing edge elliptical. There are twin fins and rudders. Tricycle landing gear retracts.

HE 280

JET-PROPELLED TURBINE-TYPE FIGHTER

Mfr. **HEINKEL** _____ Crew **ONE** _____

Duty **FIGHTING** _____

PERFORMANCE

Max. emergency speeds _____ m. p. h. @ S. L.; _____ m. p. h. @ _____ ft. alt.; _____ m. p. h. @ _____ ft.alt.
Max. continuous speeds _____ m. p. h. @ S. L.; _____ m. p. h. @ _____ ft. alt.; _____ m. p. h. @ _____ ft. alt.
Cruising speeds: Normal _____ m. p. h.; _____ economical _____ m. p. h.; _____ each at _____ ft. altitude.
Climb: To _____ ft. alt. in _____ min.; rate _____ ft./min. at _____ ft. altitude.
Service ceilings: Normal load _____ ft.; max. bomb/fuel load _____ ft.; min. fuel/no bombs _____ ft.
Fuel: { U. S. gal.: Normal _____ ; max. _____ Take-off, in calm air _____ ft.
{ Imp. gal.: Normal _____ ; max. _____ Take-off, over 50 ft. obstacle _____ ft.

RANGES

Speeds	With Normal Fuel/Bomb Load _____ U. S. gal. and _____ lb. bombs	With Max. Bomb Load and _____ U. S. gal.	With Max. Fuel Load and _____ lb. Bombs
Economical cruising speed	_____ miles	_____ miles	_____ miles
Normal cruising speed	_____ miles	_____ miles	_____ miles
Maximum continuous speed	_____ miles	_____ miles	_____ miles
*Typical tactical speeds	_____ miles	_____ miles	_____ miles

*Ref.: p. 4. Para. 2.

POWER PLANT

No. engines **2** , rated _____ hp., each at _____ ft. alt., with _____ r. p. m. and _____ in. Hg.

Description **Two turbine-type jet propulsion units** _____

Specifications	Supercharger	Propeller	Fuel
Bore _____ in. Dry Wgt. _____ lbs.	No. Speeds _____	Mfr. _____	Rating _____ octane
Stroke _____ in. Red. Gear _____ : _____	No. Stages _____	No. Blades _____	Inlet System: _____
Displ. _____ cu. in. Eng. Diam. _____ in.	Ratios _____	Diam. _____ ft., _____ in. _____	
Comp. Ratio __ : __ Eng. Length _____ in.	Impeller Diam. _____ in.	Pitch Control _____	

ARMAMENT

(F—fixed.   M—free.)

For'd fuselage _____
_____
For'd wings _____
Through hub _____
Dorsal _____
Lateral _____
Ventral _____
Tail _____

BOMB/FREIGHT LOAD

Normal load _____ kg., _____ lb.
Max. load _____ kg., _____ lb.
Typical stowage _____
_____
_____
Alternate stowage _____
_____
_____
Freight _____ lb.
Troops _____

ARMOR

Frontal _____
Windshield _____
Pilot's seat _____
Dorsal _____
Lateral _____
Ventral _____
Bulkhead _____
_____
Engine _____

SPECIFICATIONS

Materials _____
Span (est) 39'-4" Length (est) 34'-2" Height _____ Gross wing area _____ Tail span _____

Weights: Landing _____ lb.; normal load _____ lb.; max. load _____ lb.

ADDITIONAL TECHNICAL DATA

DESCRIPTION

16—38365-1

Mfr._____ Crew_____

Duty_____

PERFORMANCE

Max. emergency speeds_____ m. p. h. @ S. L.;_____ m. p. h. @_____ ft. alt.;_____ m. p. h. @_____ ft.alt.

Max. continuous speeds_____ m. p. h. @ S. L.;_____ m. p. h. @_____ ft. alt.;_____ m. p. h. @_____ ft. alt.

Cruising speeds: Normal_____ m. p. h.;____ economical_____ m. p. h.;____ each at_____ ft. altitude.

Climb: To_____ ft. alt. in_____ min.; rate_____ ft./min. at_____ ft. altitude.

Service ceilings: Normal load_____ ft.; max. bomb/fuel load_____ ft.; min. fuel/no bombs_____ ft.

Fuel: { U. S. gal.: Normal_____ ; max._____ Take-off, in calm air_____ ft.

{ Imp. gal.: Normal_____ ; max._____ Take-off, over 50 ft. obstacle_____ ft.

RANGES

Speeds	With Normal Fuel/Bomb Load U. S. gal. and_____ lb. bombs	With Max. Bomb Load and_____ U. S. gal.	With Max. Fuel Load and_____ lb. Bombs
Economical cruising speed	_____ miles	_____ miles	_____ miles
Normal cruising speed	_____ miles	_____ miles	_____ miles
Maximum continuous speed	_____ miles	_____ miles	_____ miles
*Typical tactical speeds	_____ miles	_____ miles	_____ miles

*Ref.: p. 4. Para. 2.

POWER PLANT

No. engines_____ , rated_____ hp., each at_____ ft. alt., with_____ r. p. m. and_____ in. Hg.

Description_____

Specifications		Supercharger	Propeller	Fuel
Bore_____ in.	Dry Wgt._____ lbs.	No. Speeds_____	Mfr._____	Rating_____ octane
Stroke_____ in.	Red. Gear____ :____	No. Stages_____	No. Blades_____	Inlet System:_____
Displ._____ cu. in.	Eng. Diam._____ in.	Ratios_____	Diam.____ ft.,____ in._____	
Comp. Ratio ___ :_____	Eng. Length_____ in.	Impeller Diam._____ in.	Pitch Control_____	

ARMAMENT

(F—fixed. M—free.)

For'd fuselage_____

_____

For'd wings_____

Through hub_____

Dorsal_____

Lateral_____

Ventral_____

Tail_____

BOMB/FREIGHT LOAD

Normal load_____ kg.,_____ lb.

Max. load_____ kg.,_____ lb.

Typical stowage_____

_____

Alternate stowage_____

_____

_____

Freight_____ lb.

Troops_____

ARMOR

Frontal_____

Windshield_____

Pilot's seat_____

Dorsal_____

Lateral_____

Ventral_____

Bulkhead_____

Engine_____

SPECIFICATIONS

Materials_____

Span_____ Length_____ Height_____ Gross wing area_____ Tail span_____

Weights: Landing_____ lb.; normal load_____ lb.; max. load_____ lb.

ADDITIONAL TECHNICAL DATA

_____

_____

_____

_____

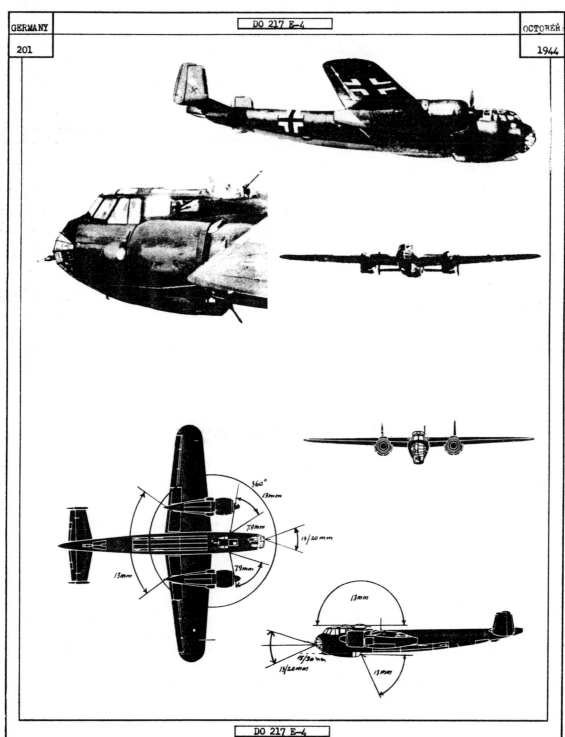

DO 217 E-4

DESCRIPTION

The Do 217 E-4 is one of the older sub-types of the well-known Do 217 bomber. It was developed from the Do 17Z (Do 215) series.

It is a twin-engine, shoulder-wing monoplane. Wing tapers moderately to rounded tips. Ailerons are slotted and split flaps are fitted. The cockpit, which houses all of the crew, is forward of the leading edge. Aft portion of the fuselage is rounded. There are twin fins and rudders, the former being slotted for single-engine control. Landing gear retracts rearward into nacelles; tailwheel retracts. A jettisonable umbrella-shaped dive brake was provided at one time for the tail; wing dive brakes may be fitted instead.

TWIN-ENGINE BOMBER

Mfr. DORNIER   Crew FOUR

Duty BOMBING (INCL. DIVE), TORPEDO-DROPPING, MINE LAYING, POSSIBLE GLIDER TUG

PERFORMANCE

Max. emergency speeds___270___ m. p. h. @ S. L.;___305___ m. p. h. @ 18,000 ft. alt.;_____ m. p. h. @_____ ft.alt.

Max. continuous speeds_____ m. p. h. @ S. L.;_____ m. p. h. @_____ ft. alt.;_____ m. p. h. @_____ ft. alt.

Cruising speeds: Normal___240___ m. p. h.;___economical 210___ m. p. h.;___each at___15,000_____ ft. altitude.

Climb: To___15,000___ ft. alt. in 15.75___ min.; rate_____ ft./min. rate_____ ft. altitude.

Service ceilings: Normal load 21,500_____ ft.; max. bomb/fuel load 20,500_____ ft.; min. fuel/no bombs 29,500___ ft.

Fuel: U. S. gal.: Normal___783___; max.___1,657___ Take-off, in calm air_____ ft.

Fuel: Imp. gal.: Normal___650___; max.___1,375___ Take-off, over 50 ft. obstacle_____ ft.

RANGES

Speeds	With Normal Fuel/Bomb Load 783 U. S. gal. and 4,400 lb. bombs	With Max. Bomb Load and 783 U. S. gal.	With Max. Fuel Load and — lb. Bombs
Economical cruising speed	@ 210 mph - 1,170 miles	@ 210 mph-1,085 miles	@ 210 mph-2445 miles
Normal cruising speed	@ 240 mph - 1,165 miles	@ 225 mph-1,075 miles	@ 225 mph-2425 miles
Maximum continuous speed	___ miles	___ miles	___ miles
*Typical tactical speeds	750 miles	700 miles	1,580 miles

*Ref.: p. 4. Para. 2.

POWER PLANT

No. engines___2___, rated 1,495 hp., each at 17,750 ft. alt., with 2,900 r. p. m. and 38.14 in. Hg.

(1,595   4,000   2,900   38.14)

Description BMW 801 A/2, 14-cylinder, twin-row, air-cooled (fan assisted) radial.

Specifications	Supercharger	Propeller	Fuel
Bore 6.14 in. Dry Wgt. 2,960 lbs.	No. Speeds 2	Mfr. V.D.M.	Rating 87 octane
Stroke 6.14 in. Red. Gear .541	No. Stages	No. Blades 3	Inlet System:
Displ. 2,550 cu. in. Eng. Diam. 52 in.	Ratios 5.07 ; 7.47	Diam. ft., in.	Direct injection
Comp. Ratio 6 « 5 Eng. Length 58 in.	Impeller Diam. 13.25 in.	Pitch Control	

ARMAMENT

(F—fixed.   M—free.)

For'd fuselage 1x15mm. 250 rds(F) + 1x13/20mm (M)

aft wings poss. 1x13 in each rear nacelle.

Through hub

Dorsal 1x13mm, 500 rds. (M)

Lateral 2x7.9/Twin 7.9mm (M)

Ventral 1x13mm (M)

Tail Poss. 1x13/20mm (F)

BOMB/FREIGHT LOAD

Normal load 2,000 kg., 4,400 lb.

Max. load 3,000 kg., 6,600 lb.

Typical stowage 20x110 lbs.

4x110 + 4x1100 or 2x2200 lbs. 8x110 + 2x1100 lbs.

Alternate stowage Possibly: 2x2200 + external 2x1100 lbs.; 1x3080 or 1x3960. 1 torpedo, 1,628-2066 lbs.

Freight_____ lb.

Troops_____ _

ARMOR

Frontal_____

Windshield_____

Pilot's seat Head, 4mm; Bottom 5mm; Back, 8.5mm

Dorsal 5-3 mm

Lateral_____

Ventral 6-3.5mm

Bulkhead_____

Dinghy Recess, 5-8mm

Engine Lower surfaces, 6mm.

SPECIFICATIONS

Materials Metal, stressed skin

Span 62'-5"   Length 56'-6"   Height (est) 12'-6"   Gross wing area 610 sc. ft.   Tail span_____

Weights: Landing 22,000 lb.; normal load 32,000 lb.; max. load 34,000 lb.

ADDITIONAL TECHNICAL DATA

A fan, geared from the propeller shaft at 3 1/16 times propeller speed, accelerates cooling air. Oil cooler under leading edge of each cowling. Elaborate system of ducts and baffles. Two engine air intakes per engine under cowling. Flame dampers usually fitted. Turret is power-driven in traverse only. Provision is made for additional 15 or 30 mm fixed in nose. May have 1x20mm fixed in dorsal position firing directly upward. Assisted take-off hook fitted, also knife-edge balloon cable cutter. Reports indicate an unknown number of 350 kg (772 lb.) "circling" torpedoes can be carried. Sub-type E-5 is fitted with large, faired wing carriers for Hs 293 glider bombs. Holding 1190 U.S. gals. radius of action with 1xHs293 bomb is about 600 miles, with 2xHs 293 bombs 530 miles. Appropriate radio apparatus for controlling these bombs is installed.

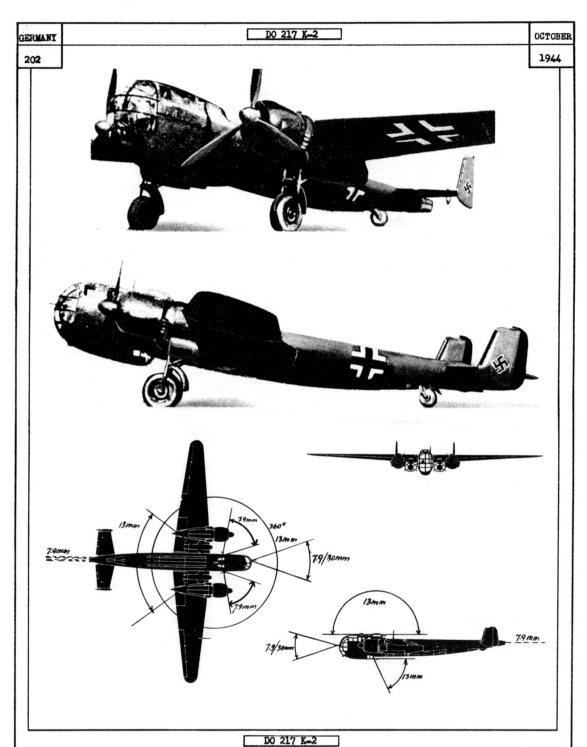

DO 217 K-2

DESCRIPTION

The Do 217 K-2 was developed from the "E" sub-type.

Its characteristics are generally similar to the "E" except for the following differences:
(1) outer portions of wing more pointed, and wing span increased. (2) nose is rounded. (3)
original tail dive brake extension occasionally modified to house four machine guns. Landing
gear retracts.

DO 217 K-2

TWIN-ENGINE BOMBER

Mfr. DORNIER _____ Crew FOUR _____

Duty BOMBING, MINE-LAYING _____

PERFORMANCE

Max. emergency speeds _____ m. p. h. @ S. L.; (est) 325 m. p. h. @ 20,000 ft. alt.; _____ m. p. h. @ _____ ft.alt.

Max. continuous speeds _____ m. p. h. @ S. L.; _____ m. p. h. @ _____ ft. alt.; _____ m. p. h. @ _____ ft. alt.

Cruising speeds: Normal _____ m. p. h.; economical 200 m. p. h.; _____ each at 15,000 ft. altitude.

Climb: To _____ ft. alt. in _____ min.; rate _____ ft./min. at _____ ft. altitude.

Service ceilings: Normal load _____ ft.; max. bomb/fuel load _____ ft.; min. fuel/no bombs _____ ft.

Fuel: { U. S. gal.: Normal 783 ; max. 1,657 Take-off, in calm air _____ ft.
{ Imp. gal.: Normal 650 ; max. 1,375 Take-off, over 50 ft. obstacle _____ ft.

RANGES

Speeds	With Normal Fuel/Bomb Load 783 U. S. gal. and 6,600 lb. bombs	With Max. Bomb Load and _____ U. S. gal.	With Max. Fuel Load and _____ lb. Bombs
Economical cruising speed	200 mph - 1,180 miles	_____ miles	210 mph - 2,300 miles
Normal cruising speed	_____ miles	_____ miles	_____ miles
Maximum continuous speed	_____ miles	_____ miles	_____ miles
*Typical tactical speeds	_____ miles	_____ miles	_____ miles

*Ref.: p. 4. Para. 2.

POWER PLANT

No. engines 2 , rated 1,595 / 1,495 hp., each at 4,000 / 17,750 ft. alt., with 2,900 / 2,900 r. p. m. and 38.14 in. Hg.

Description BMW 801 A/2, 14-cylinder, twin-row, air-cooled, fan-assisted radial

Specifications	Supercharger	Propeller	Fuel
Bore 6.14 in. Dry Wgt. 2,960 lbs.	No. Speeds 2	Mfr. V.D.M.	Rating 87 octane
Stroke 6.14 in. Red. Gear .541	No. Stages	No. Blades 3	Inlet System:
Displ. 2,550 cu. in. Eng. Diam. 52 in.	Ratios 5.07 ; 7.47	Diam. ft., in. Direct injection	
Comp. Ratio 6 : 5 Eng. Length 58 in.	Impeller Diam. 13.25 in.	Pitch Control	

ARMAMENT

(F—fixed. M—free.)

For'd fuselage Twin 7.9mm or 1x7.9/13/15/20/30mm (M)

For'd wings _____

Through hub _____

Dorsal 1x13mm (M)

Lateral 2xTwin 7.9mm (M)

Ventral 1x13mm (M)

Tail 4x7.9mm, 200 rpg (F)

BOMB/FREIGHT LOAD

Normal load 3,000 kg., 6,600 lb.

Max. load (est) 4,000 kg., (est) 8,800 lb.

Typical stowage 2x1500 FX = 3,000 kg. (6,600 lbs.)

Alternate stowage 2xFX + 2x1100 lb. 8x110 + 2x1100 lbs. 4x110 + 4 x 1100 or 2x2200 lbs.

Freight _____ lb.

Troops _____

ARMOR

Frontal _____

Windshield _____

Pilot's seat 9mm shaped to pilot's body.

Dorsal 5-8mm

Lateral Starboard, 11mm

Ventral 8mm

Bulkhead _____

Engine _____

SPECIFICATIONS

Materials Metal, stressed skin

Span 80'-6" Length (est) 56'-6" Height (est) 12'-6" Gross wing area (est) 725 sq. ft. Tail span _____

Weights: Landing _____ lb.; normal load _____ lb.; max. load _____ lb.

ADDITIONAL TECHNICAL DATA

It is probable the K-2 has been produced especially for efficient operation with the FX radio-controlled bomb. Cable cutter is fitted on nose and on leading edge just outboard of nacelles. Fixed armament in tail is aimed by pilot by means of rearward-sighting periscope. Two 2,000 kg. faired bomb carriers placed on wings inboard of nacelles with provision for heating by means of hot air from engines. Lofte bombsight can be tilted fore and aft to enable bomb to be followed during fall. 2x6.6 lb. demolition charges are carried. M-1 sub-type has 62'-5" span fitted with DB 603 engines and 4-bladed propellers. M-3 and M-8 sub-types believed to have 80'-6" span and capable of carrying either FX or Hs 293 bombs.

WITH DB 603 ENGINE

20 mm

7.9/13 mm

20 mm

7.9/13 mm

20 mm

FW 190

DESCRIPTION

The FW 190 has been used extensively as a fighter-bomber.

From a recognition point of view this sub-type is identical with the FW 190 described on page 102 except for the two following modifications: (1) the two jettisonable fuel tanks are carried by large fairings under the wings. (2) the bottom halves of the landing wheels are uncovered when in the retracted position, the fairings which are attached to the underside of the fuselage of the fighter version having been removed. Other minor changes include stiffening of wings by light alloy strips between the ribs and reinforcing of the rear fuselage near the stabilizer.

FW 190

SINGLE-ENGINE FIGHTER-BOMBER

Mfr. FOCKE-WULF   Crew ONE

Duty BOMBING, GROUND ATTACK

PERFORMANCE

Max. emergency speeds 320 m. p. h. @ S. L.; 370 m. p. h. @ 19,000 ft. alt.; _____ m. p. h. @ _____ ft.alt.

Max. continuous speeds _____ m. p. h. @ _____ m. p. h. @ _____ ft. alt.; _____ m. p. h. @ _____ ft. alt.

Cruising speeds: Normal 310 m. p. h.; economical 220 m. p. h.; each at 18,500 ft. altitude.

Climb: To 18,000 ft. alt. in 8.5 min.; rate _____ ft./min. at _____ ft. altitude.

Service ceilings: Normal load 31,500 ft.; max. bomb/fuel load 28,500 ft.; min. fuel/no bombs 38,000 ft.

Fuel: U. S. gal.: Normal 139 ; max. 295 Take-off, in calm air _____ ft.

Imp. gal.: Normal 115 ; max. 245 Take-off, over 50 ft. obstacle 2,175 ft.

RANGES

Speeds	With Normal Fuel/Bomb Load _____ U. S. gal. and _____ lb. bombs	With Max. Bomb Load and 139 U. S. gal.	With Max. Fuel Load and 550 lb. Bombs
Economical cruising speed	_____ miles	220 mph—465 miles	220 mph—960 miles
Normal cruising speed	_____ miles	310 mph—410 miles	270 mph—870 miles
Maximum continuous speed	_____ miles	_____ miles	_____ miles
* Typical tactical speeds	_____ miles	_____ miles	_____ miles

*Ref.: p. 4. Para. 2.

POWER PLANT

	1,755	3,250	2,700	41.0

No. engines 1 , rated 1,530 hp., each at 20,000 ft. alt., with 2,700 r. p. m. and 41.0 in. Hg.

Description BMW 801 D, 14-cylinder, twin-row, air-cooled (fan assisted) radial

Specifications	Supercharger	Propeller	Fuel
Bore 6.14 in. Dry Wgt. 2,960 lbs.	No. Speeds 2	Mfr. V.D.M.	Rating C-3, 100 octane
Stroke 6.14 in. Red. Gear .541	No. Stages _____	No. Blades 3	Inlet System: Direct
Displ. 2,550 cu. in. Eng. Diam. 52 in.	Ratios 5.31 ; 8.32	Diam 10 ft.,10 in.	injection
Comp. Ratio 7 : 1 Eng. Length _____ in.	Impeller Diam. 13.25 in.	Pitch Control _____	

ARMAMENT

(F—fixed.   M—free.)

For'd fuselage 2x7.9/13mm (F)
1000 rpg
For'd wings 2/4x20mm (F)
200 - 230 rpg
Through hub _____
Dorsal _____
Lateral _____
Ventral _____
Tail _____

BOMB/FREIGHT LOAD

Normal load 250 kg., 550 lb.
Max. load 500 kg., 1,100 lb.
Typical stowage _____
1x550 lbs
Alternate stowage 1 x 1100 lbs
96x4.4 or 4x110 lbs.
Unconfirmed, 1x2200 lbs
Freight _____ lb.
Troops _____

ARMOR

Frontal _____
Windshield 1 3/4" b.p. glass
Pilot's seat Head, shoulders
13mm; back, 6-8mm
Dorsal _____
Lateral _____
Ventral 6mm
Bulkhead _____
Wheel spats, 6mm
Engine Cowling, 3-6mm.

SPECIFICATIONS

Materials Metal, stressed skin. A-4/U-8 has reinforced wing and fuselage

Span 34'-6"   Length 29'-5"   Height 11'-6"   Gross wing area 197 sq. ft.   Tail span _____

Weights: Landing 7,500 lb.; normal load 9,800 lb.; max. load 10,350 lb.

ADDITIONAL TECHNICAL DATA

Master control for boost, mixture ignition, propeller pitch and throttle. Cooling fan runs at 3 1/16 propeller speed. A-4/U-8 and G-3 sub-types have only wing root 20mm's. Bomb carrier below fuselage only. GM-1 power-boosting equipment can be fitted for short emergency acceleration at altitude. Sub-type A-3/R-6 has 4x151/20mm plus 2x13mm. 28 gal. tank containing power-boosting liquid, probably "MW-50" methanol, and provision for camera in bottom of fuselage to the rear of the pilot. Oxygen bottles are mounted on both sides above camera hole. An A-5/U-8 sub-type believed to be able to carry 2x110 lbs or 1x550 lb bomb under each wing at strong points in addition to fuselage bomb, total load being 2,200 lbs.

FW 200C

DESCRIPTION

The FW 200C is the military version of the original Kondor civil transport which first appeared in service in 1937. It is mainly used for long range patrol operations over convoy routes in liaison with other bomber units and submarines.

It is a four-engine, low-wing monoplane. "Kinked" center section of wing carries the engines. Split flaps and slotted ailerons are fitted. The pilot's cockpit is well forward. A long, external, off-center bomb compartment with gun positions front and rear is on the underside of the fuselage. There is a single fin and rudder. Landing gear consists of four main wheels in two pairs, each pair retracting forward into an inboard nacelle. Tailwheel is semi-retractable.

FW 200C

"KURIER" FOUR-ENGINE BOMBER

Mfr. FOCKE-WULF   Crew FIVE TO SEVEN

Duty COOPERATION WITH U-BOATS, MINE LAYING, TORPEDO DROPPING, BOMBING

PERFORMANCE

Max. emergency speeds 217 m. p. h. @ S. L.; 240 m. p. h. @ 13,000 ft. alt.; 220 m. p. h. @ 20,000 ft. alt.

Max. continuous speeds _____ m. p. h. @ S. L.; _____ m. p. h. @ _____ ft. alt.; _____ m. p. h. @ _____ ft. alt.

Cruising speeds: Normal 212 m. p. h.; economical 165 m. p. h.; each at 16,000 ft. altitude.

Climb: To 16,000 ft. alt. in 25.5 min.; rate _____ ft./min. at _____ ft. altitude.

Service ceilings: Normal load 20,500 ft.; max. bomb/fuel load 19,500 ft.; min. fuel/no bombs 28,000 ft.

Fuel: { U. S. gal.: Normal 2078 ; max. 2567 Take-off, in calm air _____ ft.

{ Imp. gal.: Normal 1716 ; max. 2130 Take-off, over 50 ft. obstacle 3,000 ft.

RANGES

Speeds	With Normal Fuel/Bomb Load 2078 U. S. gal. and 3,600 lb. bombs	With Max. Bomb Load and 916 U. S. gal.	With Max. Fuel Load and _____ lb. Bombs
Economical cruising speed	@ 165 mph—2,150 miles	@ 161 mph—830 miles	@ 165 mph—2700 miles
Normal cruising speed	@ 212 mph—1,870 miles	@ 206 mph—740 miles	@ 212 mph—2350 miles
Maximum continuous speed	_____ miles	_____ miles	_____ miles
* Typical tactical speeds	_____ miles	_____ miles	_____ miles

*Ref.: p. 4. Para. 2.

POWER PLANT

No. engines 4 , rated 940 hp., each at 12,000 ft. alt., with 2,500 r. p. m. and 43.35 in. Hg.

(1,000   2,300   2,500)

Description Bramo "Fafnir" 323R, 9-cylinder, air-cooled radials

Specifications		Supercharger	Propeller	Fuel
Bore 6.06 in.	Dry Wgt. 1,320 lbs.	No. Speeds 2	Mfr. _____	Rating 87 octane
Stroke 6.3 in.	Red. Gear :621	No. Stages _____	No. Blades 3	Inlet System: _____
Displ. 1,636 cu. in.	Eng. Diam. 55.5 in.	Ratios 9.6 : 12.4	Diam. _____ ft., _____ in.	Direct injection
Comp. Ratio 6.23	Eng. Length 67.5 in.	Impeller Diam. 9.92 in.	Pitch Control _____	

ARMAMENT

(F—fixed. M—free.)
(All free)

For'd fuselage _____

For'd wings _____

_____

Dorsal, Fwd, 1x15/20mm
Aft 1 x 13mm

Lateral 2/4x7.9 or 2x13mm

Ventral Fwd, 1x15/20mm
aft 1x7.9/13 or 20mm

BOMB/FREIGHT LOAD

Normal load 1,630 kg., 3,600 lb.

Max. load 4,900 kg., 10,800 lb.

Typical stowage
1x550 (cement) + external 4x550 lbs.
2x1100 + external 4x1100 lbs.

Alternate stowage Torpedoes, 2x1628 + 3960 lbs.
4x1100 + 2 x 3080 lb. mines.
2xHs293, 1760 lbs each

Freight _____ lb.

Troops 25 to 30 men

ARMOR

Frontal 8 mm

Windshield _____

Pilot's seat Back, 8mm
Below, 8mm

Dorsal Front & rear, 8mm

Lateral _____

Ventral Front & rear, 8mm

Bulkhead _____

Rear gunner, 12mm

Engine _____

SPECIFICATIONS

Materials Metal, stressed skin, fabric

Span 107'-7" Length 78'-2" Height 20'-7" Gross wing area 1,270 sq. ft. Tail span _____

Weights: Landing 33,000 lb.; normal load 50,000 lb.; max. load _____ lb.

ADDITIONAL TECHNICAL DATA

Forward dorsal turret is hydraulically-operated; aft dorsal position is manual. Internal stowage in long underslung "bola" with gun positions at either end. External stowage in tails of outboard nacelles; additional external carriers outboard of these nacelles. Torpedoes, if carried, are on outer carriers.

7.9/20 mm

13 mm

TOP TURRET

13 mm

7.9/20 mm

TWIN 7.9 mm

HE 111

DESCRIPTION

The He 111 was originally built in 1935 as a transport for Lufthansa. The early bomber type was used in the Spanish Civil War. Although it is becoming obsolescent, considerable numbers probably will be used as night bombers, glider tugs and transports.

It is a twin-engine, low-wing monoplane. Engine nacelles are placed at extremities of center section which has straight leading edge, cut-out trailing edge. Outer wing sections are tapered. The slotted flaps are hydraulically operated. Ailerons are "drooping" in appearance. The fuselage is of oval section with a transparent nose of asymmetrical design. The single fin and rudder and the horizontal stabilizer are elliptical in shape. Landing gear retracts rearward into nacelles. Tailwheel is semi-retractable.

HE 111

TWIN-ENGINE BOMBER

Mfr. HEINKEL   Crew FIVE TO SIX

Duty BOMBING, TORPEDO-DROPPING, RECONNAISSANCE, GLIDER TUG, TRANSPORT

PERFORMANCE

Max. emergency speeds 230 m. p. h. @ S. L.; 252 m. p. h. @ 14,000 ft. alt.; 237 m. p. h. @ 20,000 ft.alt.
Max. continuous speeds ___ m. p. h. @ S. L.; ___ m. p. h. @ ___ ft. alt.; ___ m. p. h. @ ___ ft. alt.
Cruising speeds: Normal 210 m. p. h.; economical 180 m. p. h.; each at 17,000 ft. altitude.
Climb: To 17,000 ft. alt. in 19.3 min.; rate ___ ft./min. at ___ ft. altitude.
Service ceilings: Normal load 26,000 ft.; max. bomb/fuel load 21,000 ft.; min. fuel/no bombs 29,000 ft.
Fuel: U. S. gal.: Normal 372 ; max. 1,138   Take-off, in calm air ___ ft.
      Imp. gal.: Normal 308 ; max. 944   Take-off, over 50 ft. obstacle 2,340 ft.

RANGES

Speeds	With Normal Fuel/Bomb Load 372 U. S. gal. and 2,020 lb. bombs	With Max. Bomb Load and 372 U. S. gal.	With Max. Fuel Load and 2,530 lb. Bombs
Economical cruising speed	@ 180 mph – 610 miles	@ 185 mph-580 miles	@185 mph-1,930 miles
Normal cruising speed	@ 210 mph – 540 miles	@ 205 mph-450 miles	@205 mph-1,790 miles
Maximum continuous speed	___ miles	___ miles	___ miles
*Typical tactical speeds	360 miles	315 miles	1,030 miles

*Ref.: p. 4. Para. 2.

POWER PLANT

No. engines 2 , rated 1,230 / 1,075 hp., each at 1,500 / 13,250 ft. alt., with 2,600 / 2,600 r. p. m. and 40.46 / 40.46 in. Hg.

Description Jumo 211F, 12-cylinder, liquid-cooled, inverted "V"

Specifications	Supercharger	Propeller	Fuel
Bore 5.9 in. Dry Wgt. 1,440 lbs.	No. Speeds 2	Mfr. V.D.M.	Rating 87 octane
Stroke 6.5 in. Red. Gear .545	No. Stages ___	No. Blades 3	Inlet System: ___
Displ. 2,130 cu. in. Eng. Diam. 32 in.	Ratios 8.8 : 12.4	Diam. ___ ft., ___ in.	Direct injection.
Comp. Ratio 6.84 Eng. Length 69 in.	Impeller Diam. 8.91 in.	Pitch Control ___	

ARMAMENT

(F—fixed.   M—free.)

For'd fuselage 1x20mm FF (M&F) 130/150 rds + 1/2x7.9 mm(M)
For'd wings ___
Through hub ___
Dorsal 1x13mm (M) 500 rds
Lateral ___
Ventral 1xTwin 7.92mm(M)
Tail ___ 1000 rpg.

BOMB/FREIGHT LOAD

Normal load 915 kg., 2,020 lb.
Max. load 3,290 kg., 7,260 lb.
Typical stowage
        32x110 + 8x550 lbs.
   Internal (one of above loading) +
Alternate stowage 1/2x2,200 or 1x3,960 or 1x5,500 lbs.
   External 5x1,100 lbs.
      +Torpedoes, 2x1,628 to 2,068 lb.
Troops up to 16 men, 5 stretchers

ARMOR

Frontal ___
Windshield ___
Pilot's seat Back, 10mm; bottom, 7mm.
Dorsal B.p. glass, 2"; 6-11mm
Lateral 8mm
Ventral 5-10mm
Bulkhead 10mm; 8mm at bottom
Engine 8mm, oil and coolant radiator occ. 6mm.

SPECIFICATIONS

Materials All metal, stressed skin

Span 74' Length 53'-8" Height 14' Gross wing area 944 sq. ft. Tail span ___

Weights: Landing 21,300 lb.; normal load 25,500 lb.; max. load 30,800 lb.

ADDITIONAL TECHNICAL DATA

Data applies to H-11 sub-type. Ventral radiators beneath nacelles. Glare shields frequently fitted. Vertical internal bomb storage. A 250 Kg. (550 lb.) bomb is the largest size bomb carried internally Two large bombs, mines or torpedoes carried externally beneath fuselage; 5 x 500 Kg. (1,100 lb.) bombs may be slung underneath the fuselage, three forward and two aft. 1/2 x 7.9mm are occasionally fitted in the nose as well as 2 x 7.9mm firing laterally and 1 x 7.9mm fixed in the tail. Latter gun replaced by glider-towing hook when used as glider tug. Assisted take-off by winch system and rockets common; cable cutters sometimes fitted. H-20 transport sub-type has bomb chutes removed to form cabin. Nine jettisonable 550-lb. supply containers can be fitted. H-21 sub-type may have Jumo 213 engines with increased performance.

HE 177

DESCRIPTION

The prototype of the He 177 was first identified in 1940. It is known to be in service; has been used on an increasing scale for long-range bombing and anti-shipping operations.

It is a twin-engine, mid-wing monoplane. Center section of wing is straight, mounting the engines. Although the aircraft is technically 4-engined, it appears as twin-engined. Outer panels are tapered, tips elliptical. A highly-developed Fowler flap arrangement is used. These Fowler extensions are believed to cover the greater part of the trailing edge, including aileron sections. Slotted-type dive brakes are fitted on wings outboard of engines. The fuselage is of rectangular section, with corners rounded; about one-third of its length is forward of the leading edge. The single fin and rudder is angular-shaped; bottom section of rudder is cut-out. The stabiliser is tapered, tips blunt; elevators are straight. Landing gear consists of double wheels that diverge spanwise during retraction. Tailwheel is retractable.

TWIN "DOUBLED" ENGINE BOMBER

Mfr. __HEINKEL__   Crew __SEVEN__

Duty __BOMBING, TORPEDO-DROPPING, RECONNAISSANCE__

PERFORMANCE

Max. emergency speeds __250__ m. p. h. @ S. L.; __300__ m. p. h. @ __20,000__ ft. alt.; __270__ m. p. h. @ __5,000__ ft.alt.

Max. continuous speeds _____ m. p. h. @ S. L.; _____ m. p. h. @ _____ ft. alt.; _____ m. p. h. @ _____ ft. alt.

Cruising speeds: Normal __260__ m. p. h.; economical __210__ m. p. h.; each at __17,000__ ft. altitude.

Climb: To __17,000__ ft. alt. in __29__ min.; rate _____ ft./min. at _____ ft. altitude.

Service ceilings: Normal load __21,000__ ft.; max. bomb/fuel load _____ ft.; min. fuel/no bombs __32,000__ ft.

Fuel: { U. S. gal.: Normal __2,328__ ; max. __3,350__ Take-off, in calm air _____ ft.

{ Imp. gal.: Normal __1,932__ ; max. __2,784__ Take-off, over 50 ft. obstacle _____ ft.

RANGES

Speeds	With Normal Fuel/Bomb Load __2,328__ U. S. gal. and __12,320__ lb. bombs	With Max. Bomb Load and __723__ U. S. gal.	With Max. Fuel Load and __-__ lb. Bombs
Economical cruising speed	210 mph – 1,150 miles	210 mph–550 miles	210 mph–3,000 miles
Normal cruising speed	_____ miles	260 mph–520 miles	_____ miles
Maximum continuous speed	_____ miles	_____ miles	_____ miles
*Typical tactical speeds	_____ miles	_____ miles	_____ miles

*Ref.: p. 4. Para. 2.

POWER PLANT

No. engines __2__ , rated __2,800__ hp., each at __17,000__ ft. alt., with _____ r. p. m. and _____ in. Hg.

Description __DB 610 (DB 605 doubled), 24-cylinder, liquid-cooled, inverted twin "V"__

Specifications	Supercharger	Propeller	Fuel
Bore __6.06__ in. Dry Wgt. __1,550__ lbs.	No. Speeds __1__	Mfr. __V.D.M.__	Rating __87/100__ octane
Stroke __6.3__ in. Red. Gear __.5925__	No. Stages __-__	No. Blades __4__	Inlet System: _____
Displ. __2,185__ cu. in. Eng. Diam. __29__ in.	Ratios __10.07__	Diam. __14__ ft. __10__ in.	__Direct injection__
Comp. Ratio __7.77__ Eng. Length __68__ in.	Impeller Diam. __10.48__ in. 12.2	Pitch Control _____	

ARMAMENT

(F—fixed. M—free.)
(All Free)

For'd fuselage __1x7.9mm, 2000 rds.__

For'd wings _____

Through hub _____

Dorsal **(Fwd)** 1/2x13 mm

(Rear) 1/2x13mm

Ventral **(Fwd)** 1x20; (Rear) 1x13mm

Tail __1x20mm, 150/200 rds.__

BOMB/FREIGHT LOAD

Normal load __5,600__ kg., __12,320__ lb.

Max. load __9,980__ kg., __22,000__ lb.

Typical stowage

__2xHs293, about 800 kg (1,760 lbs.)__

__2xFx1500 kg (3,300 lbs)__

Alternate stowage

__2x3960 + 2x2,200 lbs.__

__12x550 lbs.__

Freight _____ lb.

Troops _____

ARMOR

Frontal __5.5 – 8.5 mm__

Windshield _____

Pilot's seat __Back, sides, 8mm__

Dorsal __5.5 – 8 mm__

Tail, 5-14mm; b.p.glass 3½"

Ventral _____

Bulkhead __8mm, 2 rear cockpit roof, 1 rear dinghy recess__

Engine __oil coolers, 5mm__

SPECIFICATIONS

Materials __Metal, stressed skin__

Span __103'-6"__   Length __67'-4"__   Height __21'-11"__   Gross wing area __1,095 sq. ft.__   Tail span _____

Weights: Landing __43,000__ lb.;   normal load __68,000__ lb.;   max. load __72,500__ lb.

ADDITIONAL TECHNICAL DATA

"Doubled" engines composed of two single engines. Clutch enables one engine to be disengaged. Annular radiators with controllable gills. Four rows exhaust stubs underneath each engine nacelle. Internal bomb stowage and possibly external stowage under wing. Cable cutter is fitted to wing leading edge; leading edges wing and stabilizer de-iced by hot air. Forward dorsal turret remotely-controlled from astro-dome. With 2xHs293 bombs, maximum speed is about 275 mph @ 17,000'; cruising at 240 mph normal range would be about 2,150 miles, maximum range about 2,250 miles. A-7 sub-type reported to have DB 613 engines (doubled DB 603's) and increased span. B-5 sub-type said to have four engine nacelles, presumably for DB 603's. B-7 believed to resemble B-5 but with longer A-7 span and normal loaded weight up to 96,800 with airframe strengthened and possibly twin fins and rudders.

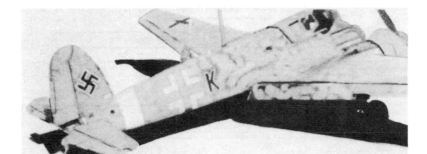

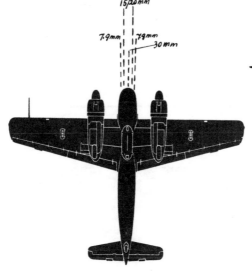

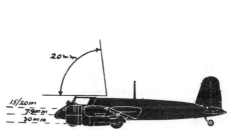

HS 129

DESCRIPTION

The Hs 129 is the specialized ground-attack airplane of the G.A.F., developed for close co-operation with the Army. It is noted for its heavy armor and armament.

It is a twin-engine, low-wing monoplane. Wings are tapered, tips slightly rounded. Fuselage is of triangular section. Nose drops away sharply forward of cockpit. The single fin and rudder is tall. Landing gear retracts into engine nacelles, a portion of the wheel remaining visible. The tailwheel is fixed.

HS 129

TWIN-ENGINE, GROUND-ATTACK BOMBER

Mfr. HENSCHEL _____ Crew ONE _____

Duty GROUND ATTACK, DIVE BOMBING _____

PERFORMANCE

Max. emergency speeds __340__ m. p. h. @ S. L.; __275__ m. p. h. @ __9,000__ ft. alt.; __255__ m. p. h. @ __20,000__ ft.alt.

Max. continuous speeds* _____ m. p. h. @ S. L.; _____ m. p. h. @ _____ ft. alt.; _____ m. p. h. @ _____ ft. alt.

Cruising speeds: Normal __216__ m. p. h.; economical __150__ m. p. h.; ___ each at __6,600__ ft. altitude.

Climb: To __10,000__ ft. alt. in __7__ min.; rate _____ ft./min. at _____ ft. altitude.

Service ceilings: Normal load _____ ft.; max. bomb/fuel load __24,500__ ft.; min. fuel/no bombs __29,500__ ft.

Fuel: {U. S. gal.: Normal __162__ ; max. __241__ Take-off, in calm air _____ ft.

{Imp. gal.: Normal __134__ ; max. __200__ Take-off, over 50 ft. obstacle __3,000__ ft.

RANGES

Speeds	With Normal Fuel/Bomb Load _____ U. S. gal. and _____ lb. bombs	With Max. Bomb Load and __162__ U. S. gal.	With Max. Fuel Load and __220__ lb. Bombs
Economical cruising speed	_____ miles	@ 150 mph-440 miles	@ 150 mph-690 miles
Normal cruising speed	_____ miles	@ 216 mph-350 miles	@ 216 mph-550 miles
Maximum continuous speed	_____ miles	_____ miles	_____ miles
*Typical tactical speeds	_____ miles	_____ miles	_____ miles

*Ref.: p. 4. Para. 2.

POWER PLANT

No. engines __2__ , rated __800__ hp., each at __8,000__ ft. alt., with _____ r. p. m. and _____ in. Hg.

Description Gnôme-Rhône 14M 04/05, 14-cylinder, twin-row, air-cooled radial

Specifications	Supercharger	Propeller	Fuel
Bore 4.80 in. Dry Wgt. 920 lbs.	No. Speeds 1	Mfr. Ratier	Rating 87 octane
Stroke 4.56 in. Red. Gear .765	No. Stages _____	No. Blades 3	Inlet System: _____
Displ. 1,175 cu. in. Eng. Diam. 39.0 in.	Ratios 8.25	Diam. ___ ft., ___ in. Carburetor	
Comp. Ratio 6 : 5 Eng. Length ___ in.	Impeller Diam. _____ in.	Pitch Control _____	

ARMAMENT

(F—fixed. M—free.)

(all fixed)

For'd fuselage 2x7.9mm, 1000 rpg.
+ 2x15/20mm, 250 rpg + (with
small bomb load),
1x30mm, 30 rds or 6x7.9mm
Through hub
Dorsal Poss. twin 20mm (M)
Lateral _____
Ventral _____
Tail _____

BOMB/FREIGHT LOAD

Normal load __100__ kg., __220__ lb.

Max. load __350__ kg., __770__ lb.

Typical stowage _____
2x110 lbs.
4x110 lbs + 48x4.4 lbs.
Alternate stowage 2x110 + 1x550 lbs.
2x110 + 96x4.4 lbs.
6x110 lbs.
Freight _____ lb.
Troops _____

ARMOR

Frontal 16mm

Windshield 3" b.p.glass,6mm frame

Pilot's seat Cabin protected front
and rear

Dorsal 6mm

Lateral 6mm

Ventral 6mm

Bulkhead 12mm

Engine 5mm behind and below, and
under carburetors, oil pump and
coolers.

SPECIFICATIONS

Materials Metal, stressed skin, flush-riveting

(est)

Span __44'-6"__ Length __33'-3"__ Height _____ Gross wing area __305 sq. ft.__ Tail span _____

Weights: Landing __9,300__ lb.; normal load __11,400__ lb.; max. load _____ lb.

ADDITIONAL TECHNICAL DATA

Air intake through air cleaner or direct from air intakes in front of engines. As an alternate to
bomb load a 30mm cannon can be carried with 30 rds, in which case the bomb load is limited to 2x110
lb. or 48x4.4 lb. anti-personnel; another alternative is 6x7.9 mm machine guns. Bomb carriers
installed outboard of nacelles and beneath fuselage. Argus engines of about 800 hp each may
replace the Gnome-Rhones. In starboard leading edge, 8 ft. outboard of nacelle, is space for
small camera. Just forward of fuselage fuel tank is a space for carrying a 2.2 lb. demolition
charge. Armament combination reported of 4x30 + 2x20 mm fixed firing forward + twin 20mm in dorsal
position, latter capable of firing forward and at angles up to nearly 90°.

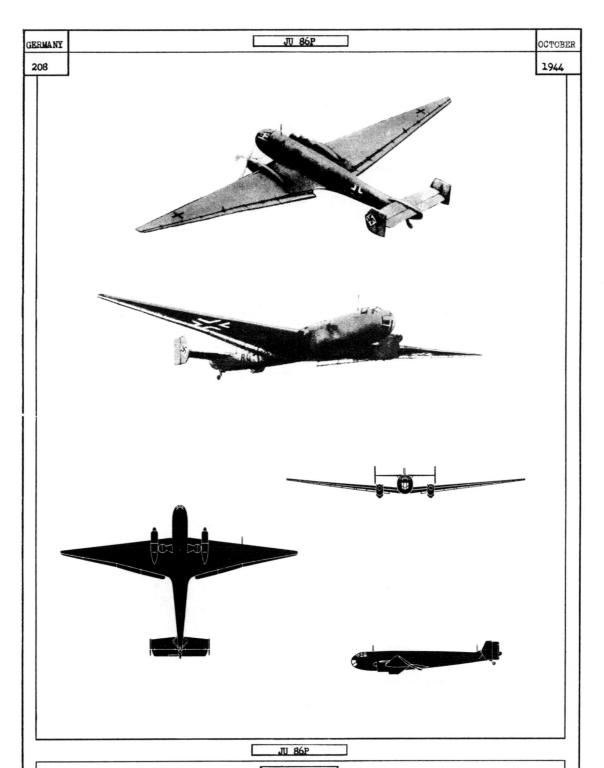

JU 86P

DESCRIPTION

The Ju 86P is a development of the Ju 86, which was originally produced both as a transport and a bomber. The P-1 bomber sub-type, or possibly the P-2 reconnaissance sub-type, has been encountered over England at 40,000 ft. and over. The aircraft appears to be the forerunner of new high altitude designs.

It is a twin-engine, low-wing monoplane. The nose is transparent and the sealed pressure cabin is short. Angular, rear-vision blisters are fitted on each side. Junkers "double-wing" is employed, consisting of four inner sections of varying camber, and two outer sections which also "droop" and act differentially as ailerons. The fuselage is of approximately circular section. Main landing wheels retract outward into wings; tailwheel is fixed.

JU 86 P

TWIN-ENGINE BOMBER/RECONNAISSANCE

Mfr. JUNKERS   Crew TWO

Duty HIGH ALTITUDE BOMBING (P-1) or HIGH ALTITUDE RECONNAISSANCE (P-2)

PERFORMANCE (est.)

Max. emergency speeds _____ m. p. h. @ S. L.; 260/290 m. p. h. @ 30,000 ft. alt.; _____ m. p. h. @ _____ ft.alt.
Max. continuous speeds _____ m. p. h. @ S. L.; _____ m. p. h. @ _____ ft. alt.; _____ m. p. h. @ _____ ft. alt.
Cruising speeds: Normal 230/250 m. p. h.; _____ economical _____ m. p. h.; _____ each at 30,000 ft. altitude.
Climb: To _____ ft. alt. in _____ min.; rate _____ ft./min. at _____ ft. altitude.
Service ceilings: Normal load 35,000/38,000 ft.; max. bomb/fuel load _____ ft.; min. fuel/no bombs up to 43,000 ft.
Fuel: { U. S. gal.: Normal (est) 584 ; max. (est) 609 _____ Take-off, in calm air _____ ft.
        { Imp. gal.: Normal (est) 485 ; max. (est) 505 _____ Take-off, over 50 ft. obstacle _____ ft.

RANGES (est.)

Speeds	With Normal Fuel/Bomb Load U. S. gal. and _____ lb. bombs	With Max. Bomb Load and 584 U. S. gal.	With Max. Fuel Load and — lb. Bombs
Economical cruising speed	_____ miles	up to 1700 miles	up to 1750 miles
Normal cruising speed	_____ miles	1400 - 1600 miles	1450 - 1650 miles
Maximum continuous speed	_____ miles	_____ miles	_____ miles
*Typical tactical speeds	_____ miles	_____ miles	_____ miles

*Ref.: p. 4. Para. 2.

POWER PLANT

No. engines 2 , rated 1,000 hp., each at 26,000 ft. alt., with 3,000 r. p. m. and 54.91 in. Hg.

Description Jumo 207 A/1, 6-cylinder, opposed piston, liquid-cooled diesel

Specifications	Supercharger	Propeller	Fuel
Bore 4.13 in. Dry Wgt. 1,430 lbs.	No. Speeds _____	Mfr. V.D.M.	Rating fuel oil octane
Stroke 6.3 in. Red. Gear ___ : ___	No. Stages _____	No. Blades 3	Inlet System: _____
Displ. 1,014 cu. in. Eng. Diam. 23.6 in.	Ratios _____	Diam. ___ ft., ___ in.	Direct injection
Comp. Ratio 17: 1 Eng. Length 86 in.	Impeller Diam. _____ in.	Pitch Control _____	

ARMAMENT
(F—fixed. M—free.)
None
For'd fuselage _____

For'd wings _____

Through hub _____
Dorsal _____
Lateral _____
Ventral _____
Tail _____

BOMB/FREIGHT LOAD
Normal load 250 kg., 550 lb.
Max. load 1,000 kg., 2,200 lb.
Typical stowage _____
1x550 lbs.

Alternate stowage _____
16x110 lbs.
4x550 lbs.
Freight _____ lb.
Troops _____

ARMOR
None
Frontal _____
Windshield _____
Pilot's seat _____

Dorsal _____
Lateral _____
Ventral _____
Bulkhead _____

Engine _____

SPECIFICATIONS

Materials Probably metal, stressed skin

Span (est) 103'   Length (est) 53'   Height (est) 16'   Gross wing area (est) 1,100 sq. ft. Tail span _____

Weights: Landing (est) 19,000 lb.;   normal load (est) 22,900 lb.;   max. load _____ lb.

ADDITIONAL TECHNICAL DATA

Ventral coolant radiators under rear of nacelles. Sealed pressure cabin automatically regulated to about 10-lb/sq.in. absolute equivalent to a height of from 10,000 to 11,500 ft. Bombs are carried internally in four vertical "Ersac" carriers. One version has a span of 84 ft. Reconnaissance version can have up to three internal cameras. It should be possible to carry a light bomb load and reduced photographic equipment. Ju 86 R-1 sub-type has GM-1 power-boosting system and increased tankage. Exhaust-driven turbo-supercharger used.

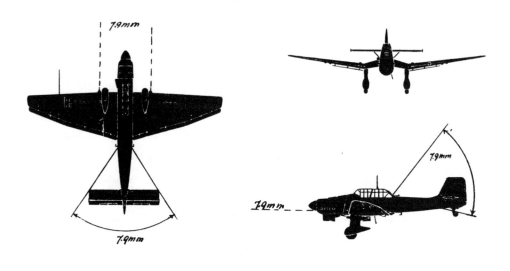

JU 87 B/R

DESCRIPTION

The Ju 87 B/R was developed from the "A" training sub-type. Although probably still in service, it has been superseded by the newer, modified D sub-type to a great extent.

It is a single-engine monoplane with "inverted-gull" wings. Center section has anhedral angle; outer panels have sharp dihedral. Trailing edges have Junkers "double-wing" feature. Fuselage is of oval section. The inclosed cockpit is over the wing, with a section of the floor transparent for pilot vision in approaching targets. The braced stabilizer is square-cut; the fin and rudder is angular. Landing gear is fixed and faired with long wheel fairings; tailwheel is fixed. Slotted dive-brakes are fitted beneath wings outboard of landing gear.

JU 87 B/R

"STUKA" SINGLE-ENGINE BOMBER

Mfr. JUNKERS   Crew TWO

Duty DIVE BOMBING, GROUND ATTACK

PERFORMANCE

Max. emergency speeds 230 m. p. h. @ S. L.; 245 m. p. h. @ 15,000 ft. alt.; _____ m. p. h. @ _____ ft.alt.
Max. continuous speeds _____ m. p. h. @ S. L.; _____ m. p. h. @ _____ ft. alt.; _____ m. p. h. @ _____ ft. alt.
Cruising speeds: Normal 200 m. p. h.; economical 160 m. p. h.; each at 15,000 ft. altitude.
Climb: To 15,000 ft. alt. in 20 min.; rate _____ ft./min. at _____ ft. altitude.
Service ceilings: Normal load 23,500 ft.; max. bomb/fuel load _____ ft.; min. fuel/no bombs 28,500 ft.
Fuel: { U. S. gal.: Normal 128 ; max. 287 Take-off, in calm air _____ ft.
{ Imp. gal.: Normal 106 ; max. 238 Take-off, over 50 ft. obstacle 1,800 ft.

RANGES

Speeds	With Normal Fuel/Bomb Load 128 U. S. gal. and 1,100 lb. bombs	With Max. Bomb Load and 287 U. S. gal.	With Max. Fuel Load and _____ lb. Bombs
Economical cruising speed	@ 160 mph – 360 miles	@ 165mph–830 miles	_____ miles
Normal cruising speed	@ 200 mph – 330 miles	@ 190 mph – 790 miles	_____ miles
Maximum continuous speed	_____ miles	_____ miles	_____ miles
* Typical tactical speeds	200 miles	_____ miles	520 miles

*Ref.: p. 4. Para. 2.

POWER PLANT

No. engines 1 , rated 1,025 hp., each at 12,500 ft. alt., with 2,400 r. p. m. and 39.3 in. Hg.

(1,180   1,750   2,400   39.3)

Description Jumo 211 D, 12-cylinder, liquid-cooled, inverted "V"

Specifications	Supercharger	Propeller	Fuel
Bore 5.9 in.	Dry Wgt. _____ lbs.	No. Speeds 2	Mfr. Ju VS 5	Rating 87 octane
Stroke 6.5 in.	Red. Gear .645	No. Stages _____	No. Blades 3	Inlet System: _____
Displ. 2,136 cu. in.	Eng. Diam. 31.65 in.	Ratios 7.87 ; 11.37	Diam. 11 ft., 5 in.	Direct injection
Comp. Ratio 6 ; 57	Eng. Length 68.7 in.	Impeller Diam. 9.45 in.	Pitch Control _____

ARMAMENT

(F—fixed.   M—free.)

For'd fuselage _____
For'd wings 2x7.9mm (F) 500 rpg.
Through hub _____
Dorsal 1x7.9mm (M) 900 rds.
Lateral _____
Ventral _____
Tail _____

BOMB/FREIGHT LOAD

Normal load 500 kg., 1,100 lb.
Max. load 1,000 kg., 2,200 lb.
Typical stowage _____
1x550 lbs.
1x550/1100 + 4 x 110 lbs.
Alternate stowage 1x2,200 lbs.
4x110 lbs + 4 clusters of 5x26.4 lbs.
each or "banded" 5x110 lbs.
Freight _____ lb.
Troops _____

ARMOR

Frontal _____
Windshield _____
Pilot's seat 8mm
Dorsal 8mm; occ 2" b.p. glass
Lateral _____
Ventral _____
Bulkhead 9mm
Engine Coolant flaps 4mm

SPECIFICATIONS

Materials Metal, stressed skin

Span 45'-2" Length 36'-1" Height 12'-5" Gross wing area 343 sq. ft. Tail span _____

Weights: Landing 8,000 lb.; normal load 10,000 lb.; max. load 12,400 lb.

ADDITIONAL TECHNICAL DATA

Radiator well forward beneath engine. Oil cooler recessed. Single large bomb carried under fuselage on ejector arms. Carriers for 4x110 lb. bombs under wing. Reported that 5x110 lb. banded
together can be carried under fuselage in addition to four wing 110 lb. bombs. "R" series designed
for rapid installation of jettisonable fuel tanks. R-2 (Trop.) has tropical equipment;
R-4 is R-2 Trop. but with protected fuel tank.

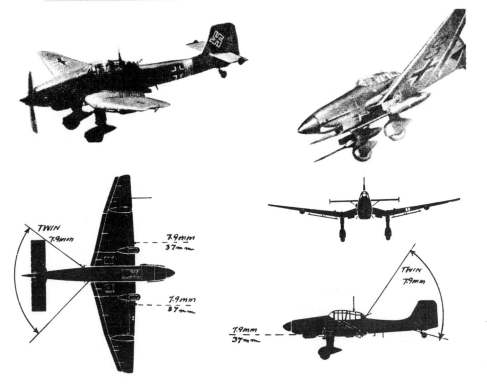

JU 87D

DESCRIPTION

The Ju 87D version of the Stuka is one of the dive-bombers of the G.A.F. and has superseded largely the earlier B/R series of the Ju 87. Modifications include a more powerful engine, greater armor, armament and bomb load, and minor changes in construction, such as the placing of a small intercooler under the engine where the large radiator used to be, engine radiators under wings.

It is a single-engine monoplane with "inverted-gull" wings. Center section has an anhedral angle; outer panels have sharp dihedral. Trailing edges have Junkers "double-wing" feature. Fuselage is of oval section. The inclosed cockpit, the shape of which differs from that of Ju 87 B/R is over the wing. A transparent panel is fitted in the floor for the use of the pilot in approaching targets. The braced stabiliser is square-cut, the fin and rudder is angular. Landing gear is fixed and faired with long wheel fairings; tailwheel is fixed. Slotted dive-brakes are fitted beneath the wings, outboard of the landing gear.

"STUKA" SINGLE-ENGINE BOMBER

Mfr. JUNKERS   Crew TWO

Duty DIVE BOMBING, GROUND ATTACK, GLIDER TUG

PERFORMANCE

Max. emergency speeds 230 m. p. h. @ S. L.; 255 m. p. h. @ 13,500 ft. alt.; _____ m. p. h. @ _____ ft.alt.

Max. continuous speeds _____ m. p. h. @ S. L.; _____ m. p. h. @ _____ ft. alt.; _____ m. p. h. @ _____ ft. alt.

Cruising speeds: Normal 200 m. p. h.; economical 180 m. p. h.; each at 15,000 ft. altitude.

Climb: To 15,000 ft. alt. in 19 min.; rate _____ ft./min. at _____ ft. altitude.

Service ceilings: Normal load 18,500 ft.; max. bomb/fuel load 17,000 ft.; min. fuel/no bombs 30,000 ft.

Fuel: { U. S. gal.: Normal 205 ; max. 364 Take-off, in calm air _____ ft.
{ Imp. gal.: Normal 170 ; max. 302 Take-off, over 50 ft. obstacle _____ ft.

RANGES

Speeds	With Normal Fuel/Bomb Load 205 U. S. gal. and 2,300 lb. bombs	With Max. Bomb Load and 205 U. S. gal.	With Max. Fuel Load and 2,200 lb. Bombs
Economical cruising speed	@ 180 mph – 720 miles	@ 185 mph–520 miles	@ 180 mph–1,220 miles
Normal cruising speed	@ 200 mph – 700 miles	@ 190 mph–615 miles	@ 185 mph–1,190 miles
Maximum continuous speed	_____ miles	_____ miles	_____ miles
*Typical tactical speeds	455 miles	400 miles	780 miles

*Ref.: p. 4. Para. 2.

POWER PLANT

        1,335   1,350   2,600   40.5

No. engines 1 , rated 1,260 hp., each at 2,500 ft. alt., with 2,600 r. p. m. and 40.5 in. Hg.

Description Jumo 211 J, 12-cylinder, liquid-cooled, inverted "V"

Specifications	Supercharger	Propeller	Fuel
Bore 5.9 in. Dry Wgt. 1,440 lbs.	No. Speeds 2	Mfr. Junkers	Rating 87 octane
Stroke 6.5 in. Red. Gear 545	No. Stages _____	No. Blades 3	Inlet System: _____
Displ 2,130 cu. in. Eng. Diam. 32 in.	Ratios 8.8 ; 12.4	Diam. _____ ft., _____ in.	Direct injection
Comp. Ratio 6.84 Eng. Length 69 in.	Impeller Diam. 8.91 in.	Pitch Control _____	

ARMAMENT

(F—fixed.   M—free.)

For'd fuselage occ. 2x12.7mm(F)

For'd wing 2x7.9/37mm (F)

Through hub _____

Dorsal Twin 7.9mm (M)1000 rpg.

Lateral _____

Ventral _____

Tail _____

BOMB/FREIGHT LOAD

Normal load 1,000 kg., 2,200 lb.

Max. load 1,820 kg., 4,000 lb.

Typical stowage _____

2x550 + 4x110 lbs.

1x3080 or 3960 lbs.

Alternate stowage 1x3,300 + 4x154 lbs.

1x1,100/2,200 + 4x110 lbs or 2x550 lbs.

Freight _____ lb.

Troops _____

ARMOR

Frontal 8mm

Windshield occ. 2" b.p.glass

Pilot's seat Head, 10mm

            Back, 4-8mm

Dorsal 5mm (in roof)

Lateral 6mm (cockpit sides)

Ventral 5mm (floor plates)

Bulkhead 8mm (for gunner)

Engine Radiators, 3.5mm

SPECIFICATIONS

Materials Metal, stressed skin

Span 45'-4"   Length 36'-6"   Height 13'   Gross wing area 335 sq. ft.   Tail span _____

Weights: Landing 8,900 lb.; normal load 12,600 lb.; max. load 14,300 lb.

ADDITIONAL TECHNICAL DATA

Induction air-cooler beneath engine. Coolant radiator beneath inner wing sections. Single large bomb carried under fuselage on ejector arms; external triple wing carriers will take 2x110 lbs and 1x550 lbs each. Air filter fitted for desert operation. Rocket-assisted take-off provision probable. "C" sub-type stressed for accelerator and catapult launch and used for torpedo dropping.

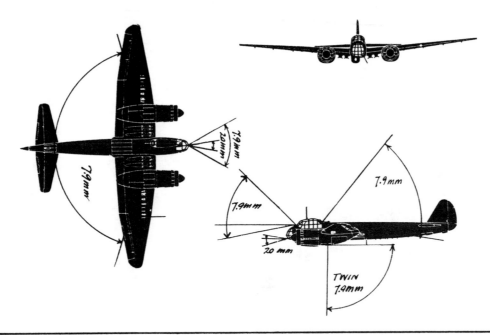

JU 88 A-4

DESCRIPTION

The Ju 88 A-4 is one of the principal bomber types of the G.A.F.

It is a twin-engine, low-wing monoplane. Wing center section is nearly straight and slightly "gulled"; outer panels are "double-tapered". Entire trailing edge is hinged, outer portions acting as ailerons and inner sections as slotted flaps. Top and bottom of fuselage are flat; sides curved. Nose and cockpit are of the angular, faceted type. There is a single fin and rudder. Slotted dive brakes are fitted under wings, outboard of nacelles. Landing gear retracts rearward into nacelles, wheels turning through 90°; tailwheel retracts.

JU 88 A-4

TWIN-ENGINE BOMBER

Mfr. JUNKERS   Crew   FOUR

Duty BOMBING, MINE-LAYING, RECONNAISSANCE

PERFORMANCE

Max. emergency speeds 242 m. p. h. @ S. L.; 291 m. p. h. @ 14,000 ft. alt.; 251 m. p. h. @ 20,000 ft.alt.
Max. continuous speeds _____ m. p. h. @ S. L.; _____ m. p. h. @ _____ ft. alt.; _____ m. p. h. @ _____ ft. alt.
Cruising speeds: Normal 254 m. p. h.; economical 198 m. p. h.; _____ each at 16,400 ft. altitude.
Climb: To 16,500 ft. alt. in 214 min.; rate _____ ft./min. at _____ ft. altitude.
Service ceilings: Normal load 24,200 ft.; max. bomb/fuel load 22,700 ft.; min. fuel/no bombs 32,500 ft.
Fuel: { U. S. gal.: Normal 771 ; max. 1,193 Take-off, in calm air _____ ft.
{ Imp. gal.: Normal 640 ; max. 990 Take-off, over 50 ft. obstacle 3,390 ft.

RANGES

Speeds	With Normal Fuel/Bomb Load 771 U. S. gal. and 2,200 lb. bombs	With Max. Bomb Load and 771 U. S. gal.	With Max. Fuel Load and 1,100 lb. Bombs
Economical cruising speed	@ 198 mph-1,310 miles	@ 202 mph-1,280 miles	@ 201mph-2,020 miles
Normal cruising speed	@ 254 mph - 1,230 miles	@ 252 mph-1,200 miles	@ 253 mph-1,900 miles
Maximum continuous speed	_____ miles	_____ miles	_____ miles
*Typical tactical speeds	820 miles	430 miles	1,450 miles

*Ref.: p. 4. Para. 2.

POWER PLANT

No. engines 2 , rated 1,260 hp.; each at 12,500 ft. alt., with 2,600 r. p. m. and 40.5 in. Hg.

1,335   1,350   2,600   40.5

Description Jumo 211 J, 12-cylinder, liquid-cooled, inverted "V"

Specifications	Supercharger	Propeller	Fuel
Bore 5.9 in.	Dry Wgt. 1,440 lbs.	No. Speeds 2	Mfr. V.D.M/Junkers Rating 87 octane
Stroke 6.5 in.	Red. Gear .545	No. Stages _____	No. Blades 3 Inlet System: _____
Displ. 2,130 cu. in.	Eng. Diam. 32 in.	Ratios 8.8 : 12.4	Diam. _ ft., _ in. Direct injection
Comp. Ratio 6.84	Eng. Length 69 in.	Impeller Diam. 8.91 in.	Pitch Control Hydraulic

ARMAMENT

(F—fixed.   M—free.)
(all free)
Ford fuselage 1/2x7.9 and/or
1x20mm
Ford wings _____

Through hub _____
Dorsal 2x7.9mm
Lateral _____
Ventral Twin 7.9mm (M)
Tail _____

BOMB/FREIGHT LOAD

Normal load 2,000 kg., 4,400 lb.
Max. load 3,000 kg., 6,600 lb.
Typical stowage
10x154 + 4x550 lbs.

Alternate stowage 10x154 + 4x1,100 lbs.
2x1,100 + 2x2,200 lbs.
Reported 2x3,080 or 1x3,960
Freight _____ lb.
Troops _____

ARMOR

Frontal _____
Windshield _____
Pilot's seat Back, 8mm
Sides, 4mm
Dorsal 5-8.5mm
Lateral _____
Ventral 5-10mm
Bulkhead _____

Engine _____

SPECIFICATIONS

Materials Metal, stressed skin

Span 65'-11" Length 47' Height 16'-8" Gross wing area 590 sq. ft. Tail span _____

Weights: Landing 20,400 lb.; normal load 28,300 lb.; max. load 30,300 lb.

ADDITIONAL TECHNICAL DATA

Internal stowage for up to 28x154 lbs, but usally only 10x154 lbs carried. Four external carriers
originally held 4x550 lbs, but now carry 4x1100 lbs or alternatively the inboard carriers under each
wing root carry 1x2,200 lb.(or torpedo) each and the outboard carriers 550 lbs or 1,100 lbs. each.
If used for reconnaissance, cameras are mounted aft of the rear of the bomb bay. A version with
2x7.9mm guns fixed on each side of the fuselage exists. With an overload of 1,374 U.S. gals of
fuel and no bombs, a range of 2,370 miles @ 204 mph is reported. Data given for A-4 applies
basically to sub-types A-1 to A-14 and reconnaissance sub-types D-1 to 6.

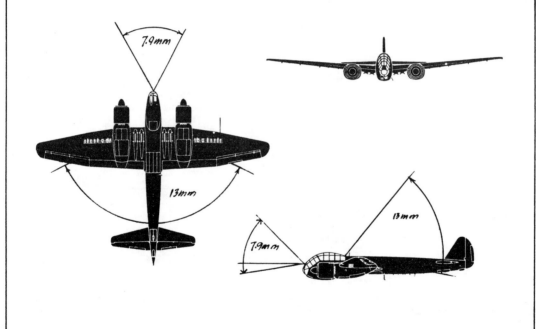

JU 88S

DESCRIPTION

The Ju 88S is a development of the Ju 88A, B and D series and probably represents a transition type between the Ju 88 and Ju 188.

It is a twin-engine, low-wing monoplane. Wing center section is nearly straight and slightly "gulled"; outer panels are "double-tapered". Entire trailing edge is hinged, outer portions acting as ailerons and inner sections as slotted flaps. Top and bottom of fuselage are flat; sides curved. Nose is rounded and of much cleaner design, no separate windshield for crew's cabin. Landing gear retracts rearward into nacelles, wheels turning through 90°; tailwheel retracts.

JU 88 S

TWIN-ENGINE BOMBER

Mfr. JUNKERS   Crew THREE

Duty BOMBING, RECONNAISSANCE

PERFORMANCE

Max. emergency speeds 291 m. p. h. @ S. L.; 339 m. p. h. @ 20,000 ft. alt.; 296 m. p. h. @ 10,000 ft.alt.

Max. continuous speeds_____ m. p. h. @ S. L.; _____ m. p. h. @ _____ ft. alt.; _____ m. p. h. @ _____ ft. alt.

Cruising speeds: Normal 288 m. p. h.; economical 212 m. p. h.; each at 18,000 ft. altitude.

Climb: To 18,000 ft. alt. in 16.5 min.; rate _____ ft./min. at _____ ft. altitude.

Service ceilings: Normal load 30,000 ft.; max. bomb/fuel load 29,000 ft.; min. fuel/no bombs 33,000 ft.

Fuel: {U. S. gal.: Normal 446 ; max (est) 1,012 Take-off, in calm air _____ ft.

{Imp. gal.: Normal 370 ; max (est) 840 Take-off, over 50 ft. obstacle _____ ft.

RANGES

Speeds	With Normal Fuel/Bomb Load 446 U. S. gal. and 1,980 lb. bombs	With Max. Bomb Load and 446 U. S. gal.	With Max. Fuel Load and — lb. Bombs
Economical cruising speed	@ 212 mph – 700 miles	@ 215 mph –520 miles	@ 213 mph–1,620 miles
Normal cruising speed	@ 288 mph – 610 miles	@ 263 mph –510 miles	@ 277 mph–1,410 miles
Maximum continuous speed	miles	miles	miles
*Typical tactical speeds	400 miles	325 miles	920 miles

*Ref.: p. 4. Para. 2.

POWER PLANT

No. engines 2 , rated (est) 1,530 hp., each at 20,000 ft. alt., with _____ r. p. m. and _____ in. Hg.

Description BMW 801 G-2, 14-cylinder, twin-row, fan-assisted, air cooled radial

Specifications		Supercharger	Propeller	Fuel
Bore 6.14 in.	Dry Wgt. 2,960 lbs.	No. Speeds 2	Mfr. V.D.M.	Rating 100 octane
Stroke 6.14 in.	Red. Gear _____ :	No. Stages _____	No. Blades 3	Inlet System:
Displ. 2,550 cu. in.	Eng. Diam. 52 in.	Ratios _____	Diam. _____ ft., _____ in.	Direct injection
Comp. Ratio _____ : _____	Eng. Length _____ in.	Impeller Diam. _____ in.	Pitch Control _____	

ARMAMENT

(F—fixed. M—free.)

For'd fuselage 1x7.9mm(M)

For'd wings _____

Through hub _____

Dorsal 1x13mm (M) 250 rds.

Lateral _____

Ventral _____

Tail _____

BOMB/FREIGHT LOAD

Normal load 900 kg., 1,980 lb.

Max. load 2,000 kg., 4,400 lb.

Typical stowage 18x110/154 lbs.

Alternate stowage 4x550 lbs.)

4x1,100 lbs.) est.

2x2,200 lbs)

Freight _____ lb.

Troops _____

ARMOR

Frontal _____

Windshield _____

Pilot's seat 5-9mm

Dorsal _____

Lateral _____

Ventral _____

Bulkhead _____

Engine Oil coolers protected.

SPECIFICATIONS

Materials Metal, stressed skin

Span 65'-11" Length (est) 47' Height (est) 16'-8" Gross wing area 590 sq. ft Tail span _____

Weights: Landing 20,300 lb.; normal load 26,400 lb.; max. load 29,000 lb.

ADDITIONAL TECHNICAL DATA

Only the front bomb bay can be used due to GM-1 power-boosting equipment installed in rear bomb

bay. It is assumed four external E.T.C. bomb carriers can be fitted for maximum load conditions.

Nitrous oxide believed used in GM-1 cylindrical tanks. This installation gives following increased

performance above 26,000 ft. for a 30 min. duration: maximum speed (with 1,980 lb. bombs and 477

U.S. gals.) 370 mph @ 26,000'; 345 mph @ 33,000'. At reduced output and 45 min. endurance: 359 mph

@ 26,000'; 327 mph @ 33,000'. "T" sub-type believed generally similar but equipped for reconnaissance.

"S-3" sub-type has Jumo 213 engines with increased performance.

JU 188

DESCRIPTION

The Ju 188 is gradually replacing the widely-used Ju 88 as the G.A.F.'s all-purpose aircraft.
It is a twin-engine, low-wing monoplane. Wing center section is straight, outer portions
tapered to pointed tips. Slotted ailerons in two sections with varying taper give a "kinked" appearance to trailing edge. Slotted dive brakes are fitted beneath wing outboard of engines. Built-
in cable cutter is placed in leading edge, V-shaped cutter around nose. Tall fin and rudder has
angular appearance. Stabilizer and elevators are straight-tapered, tips square. Landing gear retracts rearward; tailwheel also retracts.

JU 188

TWIN-ENGINE BOMBER

Mfr. __JUNKERS__   Crew __FOUR__

Duty __BOMBING__

PERFORMANCE (est.)

Max. emergency speeds __285__ m. p. h. @ S. L.; __325__ m. p. h. @ __20,000__ ft. alt.; _____ m. p. h. @ _____ ft.alt.
Max. continuous speeds _____ m. p. h. @ S. L.; _____ m. p. h. @ _____ ft. alt.; _____ m. p. h. @ _____ ft. alt.
Cruising speeds: Normal __254__ m. p. h.; economical __232__ m. p. h.; each at __Sea Level__ ft. altitude.
Climb: To __18,000__ ft. alt. in __13__ min.; rate _____ ft./min. at _____ ft. altitude.
Service ceilings: Normal load __33/34,000__ ft.; max. bomb/fuel load _____ ft.; min. fuel/no bombs _____ ft.
Fuel: { U. S. gal.: Normal __771__ ; max. __952__ Take-off, in calm air _____ ft.
{ Imp. gal.: Normal __640__ ; max. __790__ Take-off, over 50 ft. obstacle _____ ft.

RANGES

Speeds	With Normal Fuel/Bomb Load __771__ U. S. gal. and __4,400__ lb. bombs	With Max. Bomb Load and _____ U. S. gal.	With Max. Fuel Load and __4,400__ lb. Bombs
Operational speed	@ 232 mph – 1,200 miles	_____ miles	@ 232 mph–1500 miles
Operational speed	@ 254 mph – 800 miles	_____ miles	@ 254 mph–1000 miles
Maximum continuous speed	_____ miles	_____ miles	_____ miles
	_____ miles	_____ miles	_____ miles

*Ref.: p. 4. Para. 2.

POWER PLANT

No. engines __2__ , rated (est) 1700 hp., each at __22/23,000__ ft. alt., with __3,200__ r. p. m. and _____ in. Hg.

Description __Jumo 213 A/1, 12-cylinder, liquid-cooled, inverted "V"__

Specifications	Supercharger	Propeller	Fuel
Bore __5.91__ in. Dry Wgt. _____ lbs.	No. Speeds __2__	Mfr. __V.D.M.__	Rating __87/100__ octane
Stroke __6.5__ in. Red. Gear __˃471__	No. Stages _____	No. Blades __3__	Inlet System: __Direct__
Displ. __2,133__ cu. in. Eng. Diam. _____ in.	Ratios __6.86 : 9.39__	Diam. __12ft.,3__ in.	__injection__
Comp. Ratio __: _____ Eng. Length _____ in.	Impeller Diam. __10.62__ in.	Pitch Control _____	

ARMAMENT

(F—fixed. M—free.)
(all free)
For'd fuselage __1x20mm__
For'd wings _____
cockpit (rear) 1x13mm
Through hub _____
Dorsal __1x20mm (turret)__
Lateral _____
Ventral __2x7.9 or 1x13mm__
Tail _____

BOMB/FREIGHT LOAD

Normal load __2000__ kg., __4,400__ lb.
Max. load __4000__ kg., __8,800__ lb.
Typical stowage _____
10x154 + 4x550/1100 lbs.
10x154 + 2x1100 lbs.
Alternate stowage __Possibly 4x2,200 lbs.__
10x154 + 2x1100 + 2x2200 lbs.
2xFX1400 radio-controlled
Freight _____ lb.
Troops _____

ARMOR

Frontal _____
Windshield (rear gunner) 3.94"b.p.
Pilot's seat 4-10mm   glass
Dorsal __10mm__
Lateral _____
Ventral __6mm__
Bulkhead __Protects rear gunner__
Engine __Lower half oil radiators__
__5mm__

SPECIFICATIONS

Materials __Metal, stressed skin, flush riveting. Leading edge fin of plywood fabric covered.__

Span __72'-6"__ Length __49'__ Height __16'-8"__ Gross wing area __600 sq. ft.__ Tail span _____

Weights: Landing _____ lb.; normal load _____ lb.; max. load _____ lb.

ADDITIONAL TECHNICAL DATA

Top dorsal turret power-operated, aft dorsal gun in a hand-operated ring. Large "drain-pipe" flame dampers are fitted. Variation in armament may include 3 twin 13mm machine guns. Leading edges of wing and stabilizer de-iced by hot air. Early models were fitted with BMW 801 G-2, 14-cylinder radials. Five fuel tanks normally carried, two in each wing, one inboard and one outboard of nacelles and one in forward bomb bay. One or two 3 kg. (6.6 lb.) demolition charges are carried.

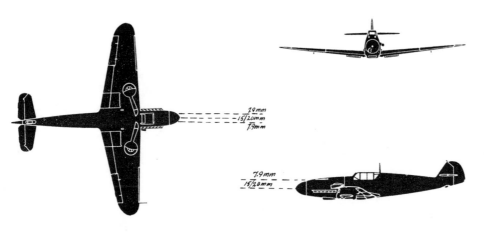

7.9 mm
15/20 mm
7.9 mm

7.9 mm
15/20 mm

ME 109 F-4

DESCRIPTION

The Me 109 F-4 is one of Germany's single-engine fighter-bombers. The tropical version, fitted with an air cleaner, was in extensive use in North Africa. The Me 109F series has been replaced for the most part by the later G series.

It is a single-engine, low-wing monoplane. Many of its structural components are similar to those of the Me 109E. Wings are of different section than those of the Me 109E and taper to rounded tips. Automatic slots and slotted flaps are fitted. Inclosed cockpit with a jettisonable cover is placed over the wing. Rudder and elevators are balanced. Landing gear retracts outward into wings; tailwheel also retracts. Stabilizers are unbraced.

BOMBER VERSION OF ME 109 F-4 SINGLE-ENGINE FIGHTER

Mfr. MESSERSCHMITT   Crew ONE

Duty BOMBING, GROUND ATTACK

PERFORMANCE

Max. emergency speeds 295 m.p.h. @ S.L.; 365 m.p.h. @ 22,000 ft. alt.; 340 m.p.h. @ 30,000 ft. alt.
Max. continuous speeds ___ m.p.h. @ S.L.; ___ m.p.h. @ ___ ft. alt.; ___ m.p.h. @ ___ ft. alt.
Cruising speeds: Normal 305 m.p.h.; economical 200 m.p.h.; each at 17,000 ft. altitude.
Climb: To 17,000 ft. alt. in 6.75 min.; rate ___ ft./min. at ___ ft. altitude.
Service ceilings: Normal load 34,500 ft.; max. bomb/fuel load ___ ft.; min. fuel/no bombs 38,000 ft.
Fuel: { U.S. gal.: Normal 106 ; max. ___ Take-off, in calm air ___ ft.
{ Imp. gal.: Normal 88 ; max. ___ Take-off, over 50 ft. obstacle 1,725 ft.

RANGES

Speeds	With Normal Fuel/Bomb Load 106 U.S. gal. and 550 lb. bombs	With Max. Bomb Load and ___ U.S. gal.	With Max. Fuel Load and ___ lb. Bombs
Economical cruising speed	@ 200 mph – 570 miles	___ miles	___ miles
Normal cruising speed	@ 310 mph – 420 miles	___ miles	___ miles
Maximum continuous speed	___ miles	___ miles	___ miles
*Typical tactical speeds	330 miles	315 miles	630 miles

*Ref.: p. 4. Para. 2.

POWER PLANT

No. engines 1, rated 1,395 S.L. / 1,220 hp., each at 15,000 ft. alt., with 2,700 / 2,500 r.p.m. and 41.04 / 37.57 in. Hg.

Description DB 601 E, 12-cylinder, liquid-cooled, inverted "V"

Specifications	Supercharger	Propeller	Fuel
Bore 5.91 in. Dry Wgt. 1,500 lbs.	No. Speeds 1	Mfr. V.D.M.	Rating 87 octane
Stroke 6.30 in. Red. Gear .595	No. Stages ___	No. Blades 3	Inlet System:
Displ. 2,070 cu. in. Eng. Diam. 29 in.	Ratios 10.07	Diam. 9 ft., 8 in.	Direct injection
Comp. Ratio 7.1 Eng. Length 68 in.	Impeller Diam. 10.25 in.	Pitch Control ___	

ARMAMENT

(F—fixed. M—free.)

For'd fuselage 2x7.9 mm (F)   500 rpg
For'd wings ___
Through hub 1x15/20mm (F)
Dorsal abt. 200 rds.
Lateral ___
Ventral ___
Tail ___

BOMB/FREIGHT LOAD

Normal load 250 kg., 550 lb.
Max. load 250 kg., 550 lb.
Typical stowage 4x110 lbs / 1x550 lbs
Alternate stowage Anti-personnel 92x4.4 lbs. Reported 1x1100 lb.
Bomb carrier(s) only beneath fuselage
Freight ___ lb.
Troops ___

ARMOR

Frontal ___
Windshield 2¼" b.p. glass
Pilot's seat Head, 8 mm / Back, 5-8mm
Dorsal ___
Lateral ___
Ventral ___
Bulkhead Laminated 20mm dural plate behind fuel tank
Engine ___

SPECIFICATIONS

Materials Metal, stressed skin

Span 32'-8"   Length 29'-11"   Height 10'-6"   Gross wing area 172 sq. ft.   Tail span ___

Weights: Landing 5,700 lb.; normal load 6,970 lb.; max. load ___ lb.

ADDITIONAL TECHNICAL DATA

Coolant radiators incorporating boundary layer by-pass, under wings. Oil radiator under rear of engine. Intake blower on left side of engine. "GM-1" power-boosting system can be fitted for short emergency acceleration at altitude.

MODIFIED FIN AND RUDDER

ME 109G

DESCRIPTION

The Me 109G appeared in service in September, 1942 and is the latest and one of the best German single-engine fighter-bombers. It is almost identical with the Me 109 F-4.

It is a single-engine, low-wing monoplane. Wings taper to rounded tips. Automatic slots and slotted flaps are fitted. The fuselage is of oval section; cockpit is over wings' trailing edge. Landing gear retracts outward into wings; tailwheel also retracts.

ME 109 G

BOMBER VERSION OF ME 109 G SINGLE-ENGINE FIGHTER

Mfr. MESSERSCHMITT   Crew   ONE

Duty   BOMBING, GROUND ATTACK

PERFORMANCE

Max. emergency speeds 310 m. p. h. @ S. L.; 370 m. p. h. @ 22,000 ft. alt.; 345 m. p. h. @ 30,000 ft.alt.
Max. continuous speeds _____ m. p. h. @ S. L.; _____ m. p. h. @ _____ ft. alt.; _____ m. p. h. @ _____ ft. alt.
Cruising speeds: Normal 310 m. p. h.; economical 200 m. p. h.; each at 19,000 ft. altitude.
Climb: To 19,000 ft. alt. in 7 min.; rate _____ ft./min. at _____ ft. altitude.
Service ceilings: Normal load 35,500 ft.; max. bomb/fuel load _____ ft.; min. fuel/no bombs 39,500 ft.
Fuel: { U. S. gal.: Normal 106 ; max. _____ Take-off, in calm air _____ ft.
{ Imp. gal.: Normal 88 ; max. _____ Take-off, over 50 ft. obstacle 1,725 ft.

RANGES

Speeds	With Normal Fuel/Bomb Load 106 U. S. gal. and 550 lb. bombs	With Max. Bomb Load and _____ U. S. gal.	With Max. Fuel Load and _____ lb. Bombs
Economical cruising speed	@ 200 mph - 550 miles	_____ miles	_____ miles
Normal cruising speed	@ 310 mph - 420 miles	_____ miles	_____ miles
Maximum continuous speed	_____ miles	_____ miles	_____ miles
*Typical tactical speeds	315 miles	290 miles	630 miles

*Ref.: p. 4. Para. 2.

POWER PLANT

	1,460	S.L.	2,800	41.04

No. engines 1 , rated 1,340 hp., each at 18,700 ft. alt., with 2,800 r. p. m. and 41.04 in. Hg.

Description DB 605B, 12-cylinder, liquid-cooled inverted "V"

Specifications	Supercharger	Propeller	Fuel
Bore 6.06 in. Dry Wgt. 1,550 lbs.	No. Speeds 1	Mfr. V.D.M.	Rating 87/100 octane
Stroke 6.3 in. Red. Gear .5925	No. Stages 1	No. Blades 3	Inlet System: _____
Displ. 2,185 cu. in. Eng. Diam. 29 in.	Ratios 10.07	Diam. 9 ft. 10 in.	Direct injection
Comp. Ratio 7 x 77 Eng. Length 68 in.	Impeller Diam. 10.48 in. 12.2	Pitch Control _____	

ARMAMENT

(F—fixed. M—free.)

For'd fuselage 2x7.9/13mm (F)

For'd wings Optional, 2x20mm (F)

Through hub 1x20mm (F)

Dorsal _____

Lateral _____

Ventral _____

Tail _____

BOMB/FREIGHT LOAD

Normal load 250 kg., 550 lb.

Max. load 250 kg., 550 lb.

Typical stowage _____
1x550 lbs.
4x110 lbs.

Alternate stowage Anti-personnel, 92x4.4 lbs.
Reported 1x1100 lb.
External stowage beneath fuselage

Freight _____ lb.

Troops _____

ARMOR

Frontal _____

Windshield 2½" b.p. glass

Pilot's seat Head, 8mm
Back, 5-10mm

Dorsal (rear) 2 5/8" b.p. glass
+ 5mm plate

Ventral _____

Bulkhead Laminated 20mm dural
plate behind a fuel tank

Engine _____

SPECIFICATIONS

Materials Metal, stressed skin.

Span 32'-8"   Length 29'-11"   Height 10'-6"   Gross wing area 172 sq. ft.   Tail span _____

Weights: Landing 5,900 lb.; normal load 7,280 lb.; max. load _____ lb.

ADDITIONAL TECHNICAL DATA

Coolant radiators under wing; oil radiator under rear of engine. Intake blower on left side of engine. "GM-1" power-boosting equipment can be fitted. Sub-types G-1, 3 & 5 have cockpit pressurizing equipment for sustained operation at high altitudes.

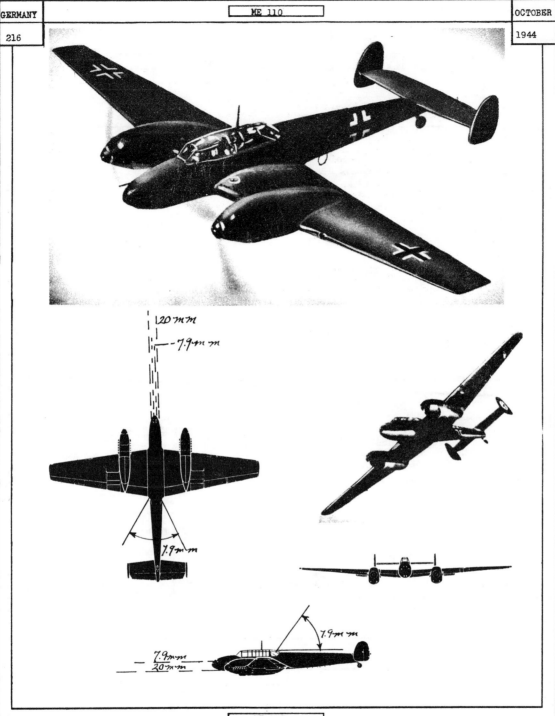

ME 110

DESCRIPTION

The Me 110 fitted with DB 601 engines was in 1939 Germany's standard long-range, twin-engined fighter. Although now superseded by the Me 410 and the Me 110G with DB 605 engines, it is still extensively employed as an attack bomber, carrying a surprisingly heavy load for its size and with special modifications for long range reconnaissance

It is a twin-engine, low-wing monoplane. The narrow wings taper to square tips, with slightly rounded corners. There are slots, slotted flaps, and "drooping" ailerons. Fuselage is of slim oval section. The cockpit inclosure is long and transparent. Landing gear retracts hydraulically rearward into nacelles; tailwheel is fixed.

BOMBER VERSION OF ME 110 FIGHTER

Mfr. __MESSERSCHMITT__   Crew __TWO__

Duty __BOMBING, GROUND ATTACK__

PERFORMANCE

Max. emergency speeds __285__ m. p. h. @ S. L.; __345__ m. p. h. @ __18,000__ ft. alt.; _____ m. p. h. @ _____ ft.alt.
Max. continuous speeds _____ m. p. h. @ S. L.; _____ m. p. h. @ _____ ft. alt.; _____ m. p. h. @ _____ ft. alt.
Cruising speeds: Normal __275__ m. p. h.; economical __200__ m. p. h.; each at __18,000__ ft. altitude.
Climb: To __18,000__ ft. alt. in __15__ min.; rate _____ ft./min. at _____ ft. altitude.
Service ceilings: Normal load _____ ft.; max. bomb/fuel load _____ ft.; min. fuel/no bombs _____ ft.
Fuel: U. S. gal.: Normal __337__ ; max. __576__ Take-off, in calm air _____ ft.
      Imp. gal.: Normal __280__ ; max. __478__ Take-off, over 50 ft. obstacle _____ ft.

RANGES

Speeds	With Normal Fuel/Bomb Load _____ U. S. gal. and _____ lb. bombs	With Max. Bomb Load and __337__ U. S. gal.	With Max. Fuel Load and _____ lb. Bombs
Economical cruising speed	_____ miles	⊙ 200 mph - 735 miles	_____ miles
Normal cruising speed	_____ miles	⊙ 275 mph - 630 miles	_____ miles
Maximum continuous speed	_____ miles	_____ miles	_____ miles
* Typical tactical speeds	__450__ miles	__410__ miles	__1100__ miles

*Ref.: p. 4. Para. 2.

POWER PLANT

	S. L.		
	1395		2,700	41.0

No. engines __2__ , rated __1220__ hp., each at __15,000__ ft. alt., with __2,500__ r. p. m. and __37.6__ in. Hg.

Description __DB 601F, 12-cylinder, liquid-cooled, inverted "V"__

Specifications	Supercharger	Propeller	Fuel
Bore __5.91__ in.	Dry Wgt. __1500__ lbs.	No. Speeds __1__	Mfr. __V.D.M.__	Rating __87__ octane
Stroke __6.30__ in.	Red. Gear __595__	No. Stages _____	No. Blades __3__	Inlet System: __Direct__
Displ. __2,070__ cu. in.	Eng. Diam. __29__ in.	Ratios __10.07__	Diam. __9__ ft., __8__ in.	__injection__
Comp. Ratio __7__ : __1__	Eng. Length __68__ in.	Impeller Diam. __10.25__ in.	Pitch Control _____	

ARMAMENT

(F—fixed. M—free.)

For'd fuselage __4x7.9mm +__
__2x20mm (F)__
For'd wings _____

Through hub _____
Dorsal __1 or twin 7.9mm (M)__
Lateral _____
Ventral _____
Tail _____

BOMB/FREIGHT LOAD

Normal load __1200__ kg., __2640__ lb.
Max. load __1815__ kg., __4000__ lb.
Typical stowage _____
__4x110 + 2x1100 lbs.__
Alternate stowage __1x1100 + 1x2200 lbs__
__4x110 + 1x1000 + 1x2200 lbs__
__96x4.4 lbs.__
Freight _____ lb.
Troops _____

ARMOR

Frontal __9mm__
Windshield __2¼" b.p. glass__
Pilot's seat __Head, 11mm__
__Back, 8mm__
Dorsal _____
Lateral _____
Ventral __6mm__
Bulkhead __8mm behind radio__
__operator__
Engine __occ. 5mm behind spinner__
protects coolant header tank
and reduction gears.

SPECIFICATIONS

Materials __Metal, stressed skin, flush riveting.__

Span __53'-11"__ Length __40'-4"__ Height __11'-6"__ Gross wing area __415 sq. ft.__ Tail span _____

Weights: Landing __14,500__ lb.; normal load __20,400__ lb.; max. load _____ lb.

ADDITIONAL TECHNICAL DATA

Coolant radiators under wings; oil radiators under engines. External bomb carriers under fuselage

and wing roots and possibly light carriers outboard of nacelles.

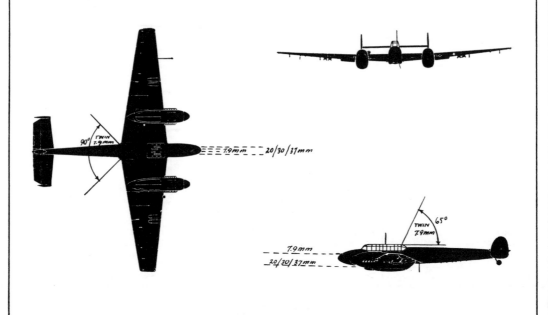

ME 110G

DESCRIPTION

The Me 110 G sub-series is identical in appearance with the Me 110 and differs only in the fitting of more powerful engines. The performance is correspondingly improved.

It is a twin-engine, low-wing monoplane. The narrow wings taper to square tips, with slightly rounded corners. There are slots, slotted flaps, and "drooping" ailerons. Fuselage is of slim, oval section. The cockpit inclosure is long and transparent. Landing gear retracts hydraulically into nacelles; tailwheel is fixed.

ME 110 G

BOMBER VERSION OF ME 110 G TWIN-ENGINE FIGHTER

Mfr. MESSERSCHMITT   Crew   TWO

Duty BOMBING, GROUND ATTACK

PERFORMANCE

Max. emergency speeds 275 m. p. h. @ S. L.; 325 m. p. h. @ 19,000 ft. alt.; 300 m. p. h. @ 30,000 ft. alt.

Max. continuous speeds ___ m. p. h. @ S. L.; ___ m. p. h. @ ___ ft. alt.; ___ m. p. h. @ ___ ft. alt.

Cruising speeds: Normal 280 m. p. h.; ___ economical 205 m. p. h.; ___ each at 18,000 ft. altitude.

Climb: To 18,000 ft. alt. in 11.8 min.; rate ___ ft./min. at ___ ft. altitude.

Service ceilings: Normal load 29,000 ft.; max. bomb/fuel load ___ ft.; min. fuel/no bombs 34,800 ft.

Fuel: { U. S. gal.: Normal 337 ; max. 576   Take-off, in calm air ___ ft.

{ Imp. gal.: Normal 280 ; max. 478   Take-off, over 50 ft. obstacle ___ ft.

RANGES

Speeds	With Normal Fuel/Bomb Load ___ U. S. gal. and ___ lb. bombs	With Max. Bomb Load and 337 U. S. gal.	With Max. Fuel Load and ___ lb. Bombs
Economical cruising speed	___ miles	@ 205 mph =725 miles	___ miles
Normal cruising speed	___ miles	@ 280 mph=620 miles	___ miles
Maximum continuous speed	___ miles	___ miles	___ miles
* Typical tactical speeds	450 miles	410 miles	1,100 miles

*Ref.: p. 4. Para. 2.

POWER PLANT

    1,460   S.L.   2,800   41.04

No. engines 2 , rated 1,340 hp., each at 18,700 ft. alt., with 2,800 r. p. m. and 41.04 in. Hg.

Description DB 605 B, 12-cylinder, liquid-cooled inverted "V"

Specifications	Supercharger	Propeller	Fuel
Bore 6.06 in. Dry Wgt. 1,680 lbs.	No. Speeds 1	Mfr. ___	Rating 87 octane
Stroke 6.30 in. Red. Gear .534	No. Stages ___	No. Blades 3	Inlet System: ___
Displ. 2,180 cu. in. Eng. Diam. 29 in.	Ratios 10.07	Diam. 9 ft., 10 in.	Direct injection
Comp. Ratio 7 77 Eng. Length 66 in.	Impeller Diam. 10.48 in.	Pitch Control ___	

ARMAMENT

(F—fixed. M—free.)

For'd fuselage 4x7.9mm + 2x20/30mm

                  (F)

For'd wings ___

Through hub ___

Dorsal 1 or twin 7.9mm(M)

Lateral ___

Ventral ___

Tail ___

BOMB/FREIGHT LOAD (est.)

Normal load 1,200 kg., 2,640 lb.

Max. load 1,820 kg., 4,000 lb.

Typical stowage ___

      4x110 + 2x1100 lbs.

Alternate stowage ___

1x1100 + 1x2,200 lbs.

4x110 + 1x1.100 + 1x2,200 lbs.

Freight ___ lb.

Troops ___

ARMOR

Frontal 10mm

Windshield 2¼" b.p.glass

Pilot's seat Head, 11mm

              Back, 8mm

Dorsal ___

Lateral 6mm

Ventral ___

Bulkhead 8mm behind cockpit

Engine occ. 5mm behind spinner

SPECIFICATIONS

Materials Metal, stressed skin, flush riveting

Span 53'-11"   Length 40'-4"   Height 11'-6"   Gross wing area 415 sq. ft.   Tail span ___

Weights: Landing 15,000 lb.;   normal load 20,900 lb.;   max. load ___ lb.

ADDITIONAL TECHNICAL DATA

Coolant radiators under wings; oil radiators under engines. External bomb carriers under

fuselage and wing roots and possibly light carriers outboard of nacelles.

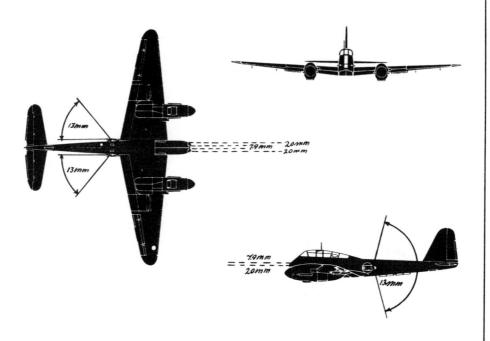

ME 210C

DESCRIPTION

The Me 210C is an obsolescent bomber that has been superseded largely by the improved Me 410. It is a twin-engine, low-wing monoplane. Wings have pronounced taper to rounded tips. Leading edge slots, slotted ailerons, and plain flaps are fitted. The nose is blunt. Fuselage is slim with humped cockpit inclosure at forward end, finishing approximately over the trailing edge. Behind this the fuselage is of small cross-section. The single fin and rudder is large. Landing gear retracts rearward into nacelles; tailwheel is retractable. Dive-brakes of extruded alloy strips are fixed on upper and lower wing surfaces outboard of engine nacelles.

ME 210 C

TWIN-ENGINE BOMBER

Mfr. __MESSERSCHMITT__   Crew __TWO__

Duty __BOMBING, FIGHTING, GROUND ATTACK, RECONNAISSANCE__

PERFORMANCE

Max. emergency speeds __315__ m. p. h. @ S. L.; __370__ m. p. h. @ __21,000__ ft. alt.; __350__ m. p. h. @ __27,000__ ft.alt.

Max. continuous speeds_____ m. p. h. @ S. L.;_____ m. p. h. @_____ ft. alt.;_____ m. p. h. @_____ ft. alt.

Cruising speeds: Normal __315__ m. p. h.; economical __240__ m. p. h.;____ each at __19,000__ ft. altitude.

Climb: To __19,000__ ft. alt. in __11.8__ min.; rate_____ ft./min. at_____ ft. altitude.

Service ceilings: Normal load __29,000__ ft.; max. bomb/fuel load __27,000__ ft.; min. fuel/no bombs __35,000__ ft.

Fuel: { U. S. gal.: Normal __610__ ; max. (est) 1,192 Take-off, in calm air_____ ft.

{ Imp. gal.: Normal __506__ ; max. (est) 906 Take-off, over 50 ft. obstacle_____ ft.

RANGES

Speeds	With Normal Fuel/Bomb Load 610 U. S. gal. and 1,100 lb. bombs	With Max. Bomb Load and 610 U. S. gal.	With Max. Fuel Load and — lb. Bombs
Economical cruising speed	@ 240 mph – 1,350 miles	@ 245 mph–1,240 miles	@ 245 mph–2350 miles
Normal cruising speed	@ 315 mph – 1,180 miles	@ 300 mph–1,140 miles	@ 300 mph–2120 miles
Maximum continuous speed	_____ miles	_____ miles	_____ miles
*Typical tactical speeds	_____ miles	_____ miles	_____ miles

*Ref.: p. 4. Para. 2.

POWER PLANT

	1,520	15,000	2,800	41.04

No. engines __2__ , rated __1,330__ hp., each at __16,000__ ft. alt., with __2,600__ r. p. m. and __37.5__ in. Hg.

Description __DB 605 B/O, 12-cylinder, liquid-cooled, inverted "V"__

Specifications	Supercharger	Propeller	Fuel
Bore __6.06__ in. Dry Wgt. __1,550__ lbs.	No. Speeds __1__	Mfr. __V.D.M.__	Rating __87__ octane
Stroke __6.30__ in. Red. Gear __.534__	No. Stages	No. Blades __3__	Inlet System:
Displ. __2,185__ cu. in. Eng. Diam. __29__ in.	Ratios __10.07__	Diam. 9 ft., 10 in. __Direct injection__	
Comp. Ratio __7.77__ Eng. Length __68__ in.	Impeller Diam. __10.48__ in.	Pitch Control	

ARMAMENT

(F—fixed.   M—free.)

For'd fuselage __2x20mm, 500 rpg + 2x7.9mm 1000 rpg. (F)__

Through hub_____

Dorsal_____

Lateral __2x13mm (M) 500 rpg.__

Ventral_____

Tail_____

BOMB/FREIGHT LOAD

Normal load __500__ kg., __1,100__ lb.

Max. load __1300__ kg.(est) 2,850 lb.

Typical stowage __2x550 lbs.__

Alternate stowage __1x2,200 + 4x154 lbs. 8x154 or 2x1,100 + 4x154 lbs.__

Freight_____ lb.

Troops_____

ARMOR

Frontal __4 and 12mm__

Windshield 2½" b.p. glass

Pilot's seat __5-12mm__

Dorsal __9mm__

Lateral_____

Ventral_____

Bulkhead __9mm__

Engine: 5mm behind spinner, rear of engine, coolant pipes 5mm above & below coolant radiators

SPECIFICATIONS

Materials __Metal, stressed skin__

Span __53'-7"__   Length __40'-3"__   Height __14'__   Gross wing area __400 sq. ft.__   Tail span_____

Weights: Landing __15,500__ lb.; normal load __21,600__ lb.; max. load __24,500__ lb.

ADDITIONAL TECHNICAL DATA

Coolant radiators in trailing edge outboard of nacelles; oil coolers under nacelles. Rear 13 mm guns in "blister" barbettes on the sides of fuselage slightly aft of trailing edge of wing. They are remotely-controlled electrically from dorsal position. A 50mm has been found on one occasion slung underneath the fuselage. 2x550/1,100 lb. bombs carried internally beneath pilot; a central carrier can be fitted between, to take an alternative load of 1x2,200 lbs. External carriers can be fitted under inboard section of each wing for 4x110 or 154 lbs. "A" and "B" sub-types have DB 601 F/1 engines.

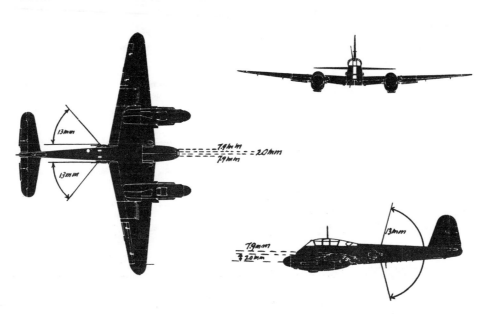

ME 410

DESCRIPTION

The Me 410 is a re-engined Me 210 as the airframes of each are similar. It is one of the G.A.F.'s principal fighter-bombers.

It is a twin-engine, low-wing monoplane. Wings have pronounced taper to rounded tips. Leading edge slots, slotted ailerons, and plain flaps are fitted. The nose is blunt. Fuselage is slim with humped cockpit inclosure at forward end, finishing approximately over the trailing edge. Behind this the fuselage is of small cross-section. The single fin and rudder is large. Landing gear retracts rearward into nacelles; tailwheel is retractable. Dive-brakes of extruded alloy strips are fixed on upper and lower wing surfaces outboard of engine nacelles.

ME 410

TWIN ENGINE FIGHTER/BOMBER

Mfr. __MESSERSCHMITT__   Crew __TWO__

Duty __BOMBING, FIGHTING, GROUND ATTACK, RECONNAISSANCE__

PERFORMANCE

Max. emergency speeds __330__ m. p. h. @ S. L.; __395__ m. p. h. @ __22,000__ ft. alt.; __380__ m. p. h. @ __25,000__ ft.alt.

Max. continuous speeds____ m. p. h. @ S. L.; ____ m. p. h. @ ____ ft. alt.; ____ m. p. h. @ ____ ft. alt.

Cruising speeds: Normal __330__ m. p. h.; ____ economical __255__ m. p. h.; ____ each at __19,000__ ft. altitude.

Climb: To __19,000__ ft. alt. in __11.5__ min.; rate ____ ft./min. at ____ ft. altitude.

Service ceilings: Normal load __30,000__ ft.; max. bomb/fuel load __28,000__ ft.; min. fuel/no bombs __39,000__ ft.

Fuel: { U. S. gal.: Normal __610__ ; max. __(est) 1,192__   Take-off, in calm air ____ ft.

Fuel: { Imp. gal.: Normal __506__ ; max. __(est) 906__   Take-off, over 50 ft. obstacle ____ ft.

RANGES

Speeds	With Normal Fuel/Bomb Load __610__ U. S. gal. and __1,100__ lb. bombs	With Max. Bomb Load and __610__ U. S. gal.	With Max. Fuel Load and __—__ lb. Bombs
Economical cruising speed	@ __255 mph—1,190__ miles	@ __250 mph—1,110__ miles	@ __250 mph—2130__ miles
Normal cruising speed	@ __330 mph—1,040__ miles	@ __320 mph—990__ miles	@ __320 mph—1900__ miles
Maximum continuous speed	____ miles	____ miles	____ miles
* Typical tactical speeds	____ miles	____ miles	____ miles

*Ref.: p. 4. Para. 2.

POWER PLANT

No. engines __2__ , rated __1,680__ hp., each at __18,000__ ft. alt., with __2,700__ r. p. m. and __41.04__ in. Hg.

Description __DB 603 A-2, 12-cylinder, liquid-cooled, inverted "V"__

Specifications		Supercharger		Propeller		Fuel	
Bore __6.38__ in.	Dry Wgt. __2,120__ lbs.	No. Speeds ____		Mfr. __V.D.M.__		Rating __100__ octane	
Stroke __7.09__ in.	Red. Gear __5175; .475__	No. Stages ____		No. Blades __3__		Inlet System: ____	
Displ. __2,720__ cu. in.	Eng. Diam. __30__ in.	Ratios __9.22__		Diam. __11 ft., 3 in.__		__Direct injection__	
Comp. Ratio __7 :1__	Eng. Length __101__ in.	Impeller Diam. ____ in.		Pitch Control ____			

ARMAMENT

(F—fixed. M—free.)

For'd fuselage __2/ 4x20mm or 2x30__ __+ 2x47mm or 1x37/__ __, 50 mm + 2x7.9mm (F)__

Through hub ____

Dorsal __2 x 13mm (M)__

Lateral ____

Ventral ____

Tail ____

BOMB/FREIGHT LOAD

Normal load __500__ kg., __1,100__ lb.

Max. load __1,300__ kg., __(est) 2,850__ lb.

Typical stowage ____ __2x550 lbs.__

Alternate stowage __1x2,200 + 4x154 lbs. 8x154__ __or 2x1,100 + 4x154 lbs.__

Freight ____ lb.

Troops ____

ARMOR

Frontal __5 and 12mm__

Windshield occ. __2½" b.p.glass__

Pilot's seat __5-10mm.__

Dorsal __8mm.__

Lateral ____

Ventral ____

Bulkhead __9mm__

__Engine: 5mm behind spinners, rear of engine & coolant pipes; 6mm above, below coolant radiators.__

SPECIFICATIONS

Materials __Metal, stressed skin.__

Span __53'-7"__ Length __40'-11"__ Height __14'__ Gross wing area __400 sq. ft.__ Tail span ____

Weights: Landing __18,000__ lb.; normal load __24,000__ lb.; max. load __26,000__ lb.

ADDITIONAL TECHNICAL DATA

Coolant radiators in trailing edge of wing outboard of engine nacelles; oil coolers in aft undersides of engine cowlings. Rear 13mm guns in "blister" barbettes on the sides of fuselage slightly aft of wing trailing edge, remotely-controlled from dorsal position. A 50mm gun has been found slung underneath the fuselage. 2x550/1,100 lb. bombs are carried internally below pilot; a central carrier can be fitted to take an alternative load of 1x2,200 lbs; external carriers can be fitted under each inboard wing section for 4x110/154 lb. bombs. Maximum permissible I.A.S. in a dive are: At 30,000 ft, 270 mph; at 22,000 ft. 310 mph; at 16,000 ft, .355 mph; and at 10,000 ft. 403 mph.

DESCRIPTION

```
┌────────────────────────┐
│                        │
└────────────────────────┘
```

Mfr._____ Crew_____

Duty_____

PERFORMANCE

Max. emergency speeds_____ m. p. h. @ S. L.;_____ m. p. h. @_____ ft. alt.;_____ m. p. h. @_____ ft.alt.

Max. continuous speeds_____ m. p. h. @ S. L.;_____ m. p. h. @_____ ft. alt.;_____ m. p. h. @_____ ft. alt.

Cruising speeds: Normal_____ m. p. h.; economical_____ m. p. h.; each at_____ ft. altitude.

Climb: To_____ ft. alt. in_____ min.; rate_____ ft./min. at_____ ft. altitude.

Service ceilings: Normal load_____ ft.; max. bomb/fuel load_____ ft.; min. fuel/no bombs_____ ft.

Fuel: { U. S. gal.: Normal_____ ; max._____ Take-off, in calm air_____ ft.

{ Imp. gal.: Normal_____ ; max._____ Take-off, over 50 ft. obstacle_____ ft.

RANGES

Speeds	With Normal Fuel/Bomb Load_____ U. S. gal. and_____ lb. bombs	With Max. Bomb Load and_____ U. S. gal.	With Max. Fuel Load and_____ lb. Bombs
Economical cruising speed	_____ miles	_____ miles	_____ miles
Normal cruising speed	_____ miles	_____ miles	_____ miles
Maximum continuous speed	_____ miles	_____ miles	_____ miles
*Typical tactical speeds	_____ miles	_____ miles	_____ miles

*Ref.: p. 4. Para. 2.

POWER PLANT

No. engines_____ , rated_____ hp., each at_____ ft. alt., with_____ r. p. m. and_____ in. Hg.

Description_____

Specifications	Supercharger	Propeller	Fuel
Bore_____ in. Dry Wgt._____ lbs.	No. Speeds_____	Mfr._____	Rating_____ octane
Stroke_____ in. Red. Gear_____ :	No. Stages_____	No. Blades_____	Inlet System:_____
Displ._____ cu. in. Eng. Diam._____ in.	Ratios_____	Diam._____ ft., _____ in.	
Comp. Ratio __ :_____ Eng. Length_____ in.	Impeller Diam._____ in.	Pitch Control_____	

ARMAMENT

(F—fixed. M—free.)

For'd fuselage_____

_____

For'd wings_____

Through hub_____

Dorsal_____

Lateral_____

Ventral_____

Tail_____

BOMB/FREIGHT LOAD

Normal load_____ kg.,_____ lb.

Max. load_____ kg.,_____ lb.

Typical stowage_____

Alternate stowage_____

Freight_____ lb.

Troops_____

ARMOR

Frontal_____

Windshield_____

Pilot's seat_____

Dorsal_____

Lateral_____

Ventral_____

Bulkhead_____

_____

Engine_____

SPECIFICATIONS

Materials_____

Span_____ Length_____ Height_____ Gross wing area_____ Tail span_____

Weights: Landing_____ lb.; normal load_____ lb.; max. load_____ lb.

ADDITIONAL TECHNICAL DATA

_____

_____

_____

_____

_____

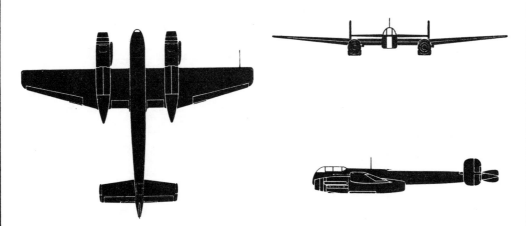

ARCS OF FIRE UNKNOWN

AR 240V

DESCRIPTION

The Ar 240V is one of the newer types of reconnaissance aircraft employed by the G.A.F.
It is a twin-engine, low-wing monoplane. Wing center section is rectangular; leading edge
is straight; outer panels of trailing edge tapered to blunt tips. Wing root fillets are small.
Fuselage is slim, with transparent cabin in nose, and it projects rearward beyond elevator; there
is additional fin area on fuselage tail cone. Stabilizer is mounted on top of fuselage. Twin
fins and rudders are employed. Landing gear, consisting of two double wheels, retracts rearward
into engine nacelles. Tailwheel probably retracts.

AR 240 V

TWIN-ENGINE RECONNAISSANCE

Mfr. __ARADO__ Crew __TWO__

Duty __RECONNAISSANCE, POSSIBLY FIGHTING OR BOMBING__

PERFORMANCE

Max. emergency speeds_____ m. p. h. @ S. L.; __370/400__ m. p. h. @ __22/23,000__ ft. alt.; _____ m. p. h. @ _____ ft. alt.
Max. continuous speeds_____ m. p. h. @ S. L.; _____ m. p. h. @ _____ ft. alt.; _____ m. p. h. @ _____ ft. alt.
Cruising speeds: Normal_____ m. p. h.; _____ economical _____ m. p. h.; _____ each at _____ ft. altitude.
Climb: To _____ ft. alt. in _____ min.; rate _____ ft./min. at _____ ft. altitude.
Service ceilings: Normal load __(est) 42,000__ ft.; max. bomb/fuel load _____ ft.; min. fuel/no bombs _____ ft.
Fuel: { U. S. gal.: Normal _____ ; max. _____ Take-off, in calm air _____ ft.
       { Imp. gal.: Normal _____ ; max. _____ Take-off, over 50 ft. obstacle _____ ft.

RANGES

Speeds	With Normal Fuel/Bomb Load _____ U. S. gal. and _____ lb. bombs	With Max. Bomb Load and _____ U. S. gal.	With Max. Fuel Load and _____ lb. Bombs
Economical cruising speed	_____ miles	_____ miles	_____ miles
Normal cruising speed	_____ miles	_____ miles	_____ miles
Maximum continuous speed	__est. endurance, 5hrs.__ miles	_____ miles	_____ miles
*Typical tactical speeds	_____ miles	_____ miles	_____ miles

*Ref.: p. 4. Para. 2.

POWER PLANT

No. engines __2__, rated __1,335__ hp., each at __18,700__ ft. alt., with _____ r. p. m. and _____ in. Hg.

Description __Assumed DB605 B, 12-cylinder, liquid-cooled, inverted "V"__

Specifications		Supercharger	Propeller	Fuel
Bore __6.06__ in.	Dry Wgt. __1,550__ lbs.	No. Speeds __1__	Mfr. _____	Rating __87__ octane
Stroke __6.30__ in.	Red. Gear __.534__	No. Stages _____	No. Blades __3__	Inlet System: _____
Displ. __2,185__ cu. in.	Eng. Diam. __29__ in.	Ratios __10.07__	Diam. _____ ft., _____ in.	__Direct injection__
Comp. Ratio __7.77__	Eng. Length __68__ in.	Impeller Diam. __10.48__ in.	Pitch Control _____	

ARMAMENT

(F—fixed. M—free.)

For'd fuselage _____

__Wings Aft: Poss.__
__2x13mm__
Through hub _____
Dorsal __1 or twin 7.9mm (M)__
Lateral _____
Ventral __1 or twin 7.9mm (M)__
Tail _____

BOMB/FREIGHT LOAD

__None__

Normal load _____ kg., _____ lb.
Max. load _____ kg., _____ lb.
Typical stowage _____
_____
_____
Alternate stowage _____
_____
Freight _____ lb.
Troops _____

ARMOR

Frontal _____
Windshield _____
Pilot's seat __Probably protected.__
_____
Dorsal _____
Lateral _____
Ventral _____
Bulkhead _____
Engine _____

SPECIFICATIONS

Materials __Metal__

Span __(est) 50'__ Length __(est) 38'__ Height __(est) 11'__ Gross wing area __(est) 1400__ sq.ft. Tail span _____

Weights: Landing _____ lb.; normal load _____ lb.; max. load _____ lb.

ADDITIONAL TECHNICAL DATA

Oil coolers probably under engines. Annular air inlets in nose of spinner. Reported dorsal gun (s) remotely-controlled from pressure cabin and ventral gun(s) sighted through an optical device. Aft wing guns probably are fixed in rear of engine nacelles. Pressure cabin is fitted. Crew believed to sit back to back with partition between their seats. Reported cabin roof consists of two layers of thick glass. "GM-1" power-boosting installation probably employed. Camera believed fitted in rear fuselage compartment with fuel tank in forward section. DB 603 engines may be used. It is possible that both engines revolve in the same direction and that therefore the additional fin area on the fuselage tail cone is offset and that its purpose is to counteract propellor torque during take-off and high-speed maneuvering.

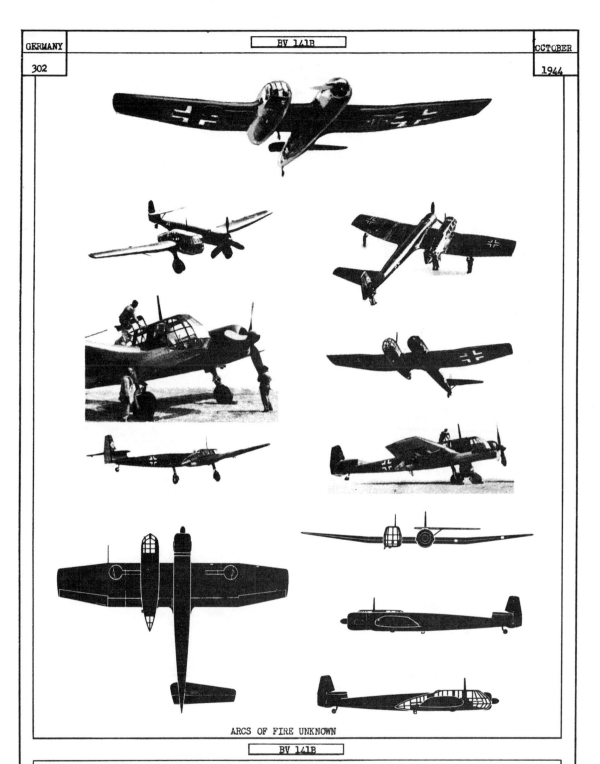

ARCS OF FIRE UNKNOWN

BV 141B

DESCRIPTION

The BV 141 was designed for tactical reconnaissance and may be in service in small numbers.
It is a single-engine, mid-wing, unsymmetrical monoplane. The engine is housed in the main
fuselage on the left wing. The closed cabin on the right wing has a large amount of transparent
panelling and terminates in a transparent gun position. Wing's center section is straight, outer
panels trapezoidal; the tips are blunt. The fin and rudder is angular-shaped. Horizontal stabilizer is placed only on port side, with a short stub on the starboard side. Landing gear retracts outward into wings.

BV 141B

UNSYMMETRICAL SINGLE ENGINE ARMY COOPERATION

Mfr. **BLOHM & VOSS**   Crew **THREE**

Duty **ARMY COOPERATION, RECONNAISSANCE, POSSIBLY GROUND ATTACK**

PERFORMANCE

Max. emergency speeds _____ m. p. h. @ S. L.; (est) 280 m. p. h. @ 16,000 ft. alt.; _____ m. p. h. @ _____ ft.alt.

Max. continuous speeds _____ m. p. h. @ S. L.; _____ m. p. h. @ _____ ft. alt.; _____ m. p. h. @ _____ ft. alt.

Cruising speeds: Normal _____ m. p. h.; _____ economical _____ m. p. h.; each at _____ ft. altitude.

Climb: To _____ ft. alt. in _____ min.; rate _____ ft./min. at _____ ft. altitude.

Service ceilings: Normal load _____ ft.; max. bomb/fuel load _____ ft.; min. fuel/no bombs _____ ft.

Fuel: U. S. gal.: Normal **(est) 140** ; max. _____ Take-off, in calm air _____ ft.

Imp. gal.: Normal **(est) 116** ; max. _____ Take-off, over 50 ft. obstacle _____ ft.

RANGES

Speeds	With Normal Fuel/Bomb Load U. S. gal. and ____ lb. bombs		With Max. Bomb Load and ____ U. S. gal.	With Max. Fuel Load and ____ lb. Bombs
Economical cruising speed	_____	miles	_____ miles	_____ miles
Normal cruising speed	_____	miles	_____ miles	_____ miles
Maximum continuous speed	_____	miles	_____ miles	_____ miles
*Typical tactical speeds	_____	miles	_____ miles	_____ miles

*Ref.: p. 4. Para. 2.

POWER PLANT

No. engines **1**, rated **1,495** hp., each at **17,750** ft. alt., with **2,900** r. p. m. and **38.14** in. Hg.

1,595   4,000   2,900   38.14

Description **BMW 801, 14-cylinder, twin-row, fan-assisted, air-cooled radial**

Specifications		Supercharger		Propeller		Fuel	
Bore **6.14** in.	Dry Wgt. **2,960** lbs.	No. Speeds **2**		Mfr. **V.D.M.**		Rating **87** octane	
Stroke **6.14** in.	Red. Gear **.541**	No. Stages		No. Blades **3**		Inlet System:	
Displ. **2,550** cu. in.	Eng. Diam. **52** in.	Ratios **5.07 : 7.47**		Diam. __ ft., __ in.		**Direct injection**	
Comp. Ratio **6 :.5**	Eng. Length **58** in.	Impeller Diam. **13.25** in.		Pitch Control			

ARMAMENT

(F—fixed. M—free.)

For'd fuselage **Probably 2x7.9mm (F)**

For'd wings _____

Through hub _____

Dorsal **1 or possibly 2x7.9mm (M)**

Lateral _____

Ventral _____

Tail **1 or twin 7.9mm (M)**

BOMB/FREIGHT LOAD

Normal load _____ kg., _____ lb.

Max. load **200** kg., **440** lb.

Typical stowage **4x110 lbs.**

Alternate stowage _____

Freight _____ lb.

Troops _____

ARMOR

Frontal _____

Windshield _____

Pilot's seat _____

Dorsal _____

Lateral _____

Ventral _____

Bulkhead _____

Possible 1/2 of tail of nacelle is armored

SPECIFICATIONS

Materials **Metal, stressed skin**

Span **(est) 60'**   Length **(est) 45'**   Height _____   Gross wing area **(est) 1,580** / sq. ft. Tail span _____

Weights: Landing **7,400** lb.; normal load **8,500** lb.; max. load _____ lb.

ADDITIONAL TECHNICAL DATA

External bomb carriers beneath wing. Gun(s) in tail of nacelle on fully rotatable power-driven cone mounting. Older "A" type had BMW 132K 9-cylinder radial of 960 hp at 2,000 ft with following performance: Climb to 5,500' in 4.5 min.; service ceiling (normal load) 25,500', (finish) 28,000; maximum speed 212 mph at 3,000'; cruising at 170 mph at 5,500' range is 550 miles, at 125 mph, 720 miles.

7.9mm

7.9mm

FI 156

DESCRIPTION

The Fi 156 "Storch" was developed in peace time. It is one of the G.A.F.'s principal army cooperation aircraft.

It is a single-engine, high-wing monoplane. The wing is parallel in chord, braced by Vee struts. An adjustable metal slat is fitted along the whole leading edge. The entire trailing edge is hinged, inner portions operating as flaps, outer portions as ailerons. Fuselage is rectangular; cabin provides excellent visibility. There is a braced tail, single fin and rudder. Landing gear is fixed and is exceptionally strong to permit heavy landings.

"STORCH" SINGLE-ENGINE ARMY COOPERATION

Mfr. **FIESELER**   Crew **TWO TO THREE**

Duty **ARMY COOPERATION, RECONNAISSANCE, STAFF TRANSPORT**

PERFORMANCE

Max. emergency speeds __110__ m. p. h. @ S. L.; _____ m. p. h. @ _____ ft. alt.; _____ m. p. h. @ _____ ft. alt.

Max. continuous speeds _____ m. p. h. @ S. L.; _____ m. p. h. @ _____ ft. alt.; _____ m. p. h. @ _____ ft. alt.

Cruising speeds: Normal __82__ m. p. h.; ___ economical __60__ m. p. h.; ___ each at __Sea Level__ ft. altitude.

Climb: To __6,500__ ft. alt. in __9__ min.; rate _____ ft./min. at _____ ft. altitude.

Service ceilings: Normal load __15,000__ ft.; max. bomb/fuel load _____ ft.; min. fuel/no bombs __17,500__ ft.

Fuel: { U. S. gal.: Normal __39__ ; max. __93__   Take-off, in calm air _____ ft.
{ Imp. gal.: Normal __32__ ; max. __77__   Take-off, over 50 ft. obstacle __690__ ft.

RANGES

Speeds	With Normal Fuel/Bomb Load __39__ U. S. gal. and ___ lb. bombs	With Max. Bomb Load and ___ U. S. gal.	With Max. Fuel Load and __-__ lb. Bombs
Economical cruising speed	@ 60 mph – 240 miles	___ miles	@ 60 mph –630 miles
Normal cruising speed	@ 82 mph – 230 miles	___ miles	@ 82 mph –600 miles
Maximum continuous speed	___ miles	___ miles	___ miles
*Typical tactical speeds	___ miles	___ miles	___ miles

*Ref.: p. 4. Para. 2.

POWER PLANT

No. engines __1__ , rated __240__ hp., each at __S.L.__ ft. alt.; with __2,000__ r. p. m. and _____ in. Hg.

Description __Argus As 10C/3, 8-cylinder, air-cooled inverted "V"__

Specifications	Supercharger	Propeller	Fuel
Bore __4.72__ in. Dry Wgt. __470__ lbs.	No. Speeds __None__	Mfr. _____	Rating __87__ octane
Stroke __5.51__ in. Red. Gear __None__	No. Stages _____	No. Blades __2__	Inlet System: _____
Displ. __771__ cu. in. Eng. Diam. __34.5__ in.	Ratios _____	Diam. ___ ft., ___ in.	__Carburetor__
Comp. Ratio __5.9__ Eng. Length __43.5__ in.	Impeller Diam. _____ in.	Pitch Control _____	

ARMAMENT

(F—fixed.   M—free.)

For'd fuselage _____

_____

For'd wings _____

Through hub _____

Dorsal __1 x 7.9mm (M)__

Lateral _____

Ventral _____

Tail _____

BOMB/FREIGHT LOAD

Normal load _____ kg., _____ lb.

Max. load _____ kg., _____ lb.

Typical stowage _____

_____

Alternate stowage _____

_____

Freight _____ lb.

Troops _____

ARMOR

Frontal _____

Windshield _____

Pilot's seat _____

Dorsal _____

Lateral _____

Ventral _____

Bulkhead _____

Engine _____

SPECIFICATIONS

Materials __Metal, fabric-covering__

Span __46'-8"__   Length __31'-10"__   Height __8'-6"__   Gross wing area __280 sq. ft.__   Tail span _____

Weights: Landing __2,250__ lb.; normal load __2,900__ lb.; max. load __2,850__ lb.

ADDITIONAL TECHNICAL DATA

"P" sub-type can be fitted with external carriers for light bombs. Can fly as slow as 40 mph.

"C-1" sub-type staff transport version; "C-2" reconnaissance version; "C-3" and "C-5" are tropical

versions. Stalling speed, 34 mph, landing speed 25 mph with run of under 100 ft.

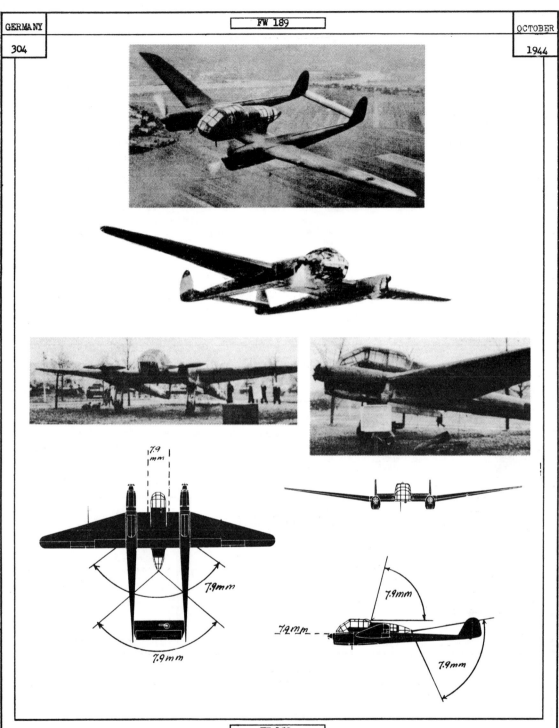

FW 189

DESCRIPTION

The FW 189 appeared in service in 1941 and at present forms a part of the short-range re-connaissance aircraft of the G.A.F.

It is a twin-engine, low-wing monoplane with twin booms and a central nacelle. Flaps are fitted on center section of wing, beneath the fuselage, and also on outer sections with the ailerons. The transparent nose is composed of flat sections. Landing gear retracts rearward into engine nacelles. Tailwheel retracts sideways into stabilizer.

FW 189

TWIN-ENGINE ARMY COOPERATION

Mfr. FOCKE-WULF   Crew BELIEVED THREE

Duty ARMY-COOPERATION; COMMUNICATIONS, AMBULANCE, POSSIBLY GROUND ATTACK

PERFORMANCE

Max. emergency speeds __190__ m. p. h. @ S. L.; __210__ m. p. h. @ __9,000__ ft. alt.; _____ m. p. h. @ _____ ft.alt.
Max. continuous speeds _____ m. p. h. @ S. L.; _____ m. p. h. @ _____ ft. alt.; _____ m. p. h. @ _____ ft. alt.
Cruising speeds: Normal __190__ m. p. h.; economical __130__ m. p. h.; _____ each at __10,000__ ft. altitude.
Climb: To __10,000__ ft. alt. in __6__ min.; rate _____ ft./min. at _____ ft. altitude.
Service ceilings: Normal load 27,500 ft.; max. bomb/fuel load _____ ft.; min. fuel/no bombs __30,000__ ft.
Fuel: {U. S. gal.: Normal (est) 181 _____ ; max. _____ Take-off, in calm air _____ ft.
      {Imp. gal.: Normal (est) 150 _____ ; max. _____ Take-off, over 50 ft. obstacle _____ ft.

RANGES

Speeds	With Normal Fuel/Bomb Load __181__ U. S. gal. and _____ lb. bombs	With Max. Bomb Load and _____ U. S. gal.	With Max. Fuel Load and _____ lb. Bombs
Economical cruising speed	● 130 mph – 970 miles	_____ miles	_____ miles
Normal cruising speed	❷ 190 mph – 620 miles	_____ miles	_____ miles
Maximum continuous speed	_____ miles	_____ miles	_____ miles
* Typical tactical speeds	_____ miles	_____ miles	_____ miles

*Ref.: p. 4. Para. 2.

POWER PLANT

No. engines __2__ , rated __450__ hp., each at __9,500__ ft. alt., with __3,250__ r. p. m. and _____ in. Hg.

Description Argus As 410 A/1, 12-cylinder, air-cooled inverted "V"

Specifications		Supercharger		Propeller		Fuel	
Bore __4.13__ in.	Dry Wgt. __660__ lbs.	No. Speeds __1__		Mfr. __Argus__		Rating __87__ octane	
Stroke __4.53__ in.	Red. Gear __.670__	No. Stages _____		No. Blades __2__		Inlet System: _____	
Displ. __732__ cu. in.	Eng. Diam. 25.8 in.	Ratios __8.73__		Diam. ___ ft., ___ in.		Carburetor	
Comp. Ratio 6.4	Eng. Length 72.8 in.	Impeller Diam. _____ in.		Pitch Control __Hydraulic__			

ARMAMENT

(F—fixed. M—free.)

For'd fuselage _____

For'd wings 2x7.9mm (F)

Through hub _____
Dorsal 1x7.9mm(M)
Lateral _____
Ventral _____
Tail 1 or twin 7.9 mm (M)

BOMB/FREIGHT LOAD

Normal load _____ kg., _____ lb.
Max. load __200__ kg., __440__ lb.
Typical stowage
            4x110 lbs.

Alternate stowage _____

Freight _____ lb.
Troops _____

ARMOR

Frontal _____
Windshield _____
Pilot's seat _____

Dorsal _____
Lateral _____
Ventral _____
Bulkhead _____
Possibly 1/2 of tail is
            armor-plated

SPECIFICATIONS

Materials Metal

Span __60'-5"__   Length __39'-5"__   Height _____   Gross wing area __409 sq. ft.__ Tail span _____

Weights: Landing 6,300 lb.; normal load 7,500 lb.; max. load _____ lb.

ADDITIONAL TECHNICAL DATA

Twin MG 81 in tail of nacelle on fully-rotatable power-driven cone. Bomb carriers under wing.
Designed for easy transport. On ambulance version stretcher is loaded through tail. An advanced
training version has special nacelle. Smoke apparatus can be installed. It is not known
whether bombs are carried as overload or as alternative to fuel or other disposable load. If
the former, the ranges would be reduced by about 10%; if the latter, by about 50%. If Ghome-Rhone
engines of 800 hp at 7,000 ft. are fitted, the performances would be increased.

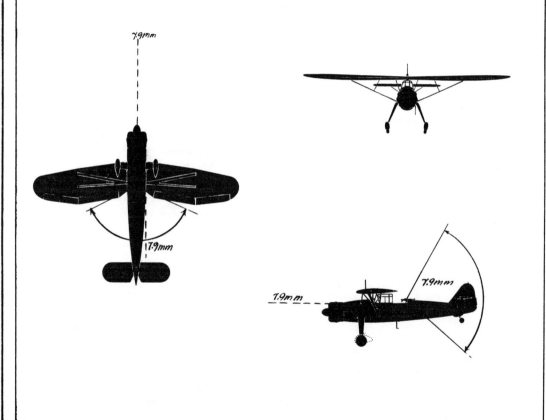

HS 126

DESCRIPTION

The Hs 126 is obsolescent, having been in service since 1936. It is sometimes used as a glider tug.

It is a single-engine, parasol-wing monoplane. Wing is carried above fuselage on two "N" struts and braced to fuselage by Vee struts. Ailerons are slotted; flaps are hydraulically-operated. Fuselage is of oval section. There is a single fin and rudder. The strut-braced stabilizer is mounted on the fin. Landing gear is fixed. Pilot's cockpit is inclosed, observer's semi-inclosed.

HS 126

SINGLE-ENGINE ARMY COOPERATION

Mfr. HENSCHEL   Crew TWO

Duty ARMY – COOPERATION, GLIDER TUG

PERFORMANCE

Max. emergency speeds __190__ m. p. h. @ S. L.; __230__ m. p. h. @ __15,000__ ft. alt.; _____ m. p. h. @ _____ ft.alt.
Max. continuous speeds _____ m. p. h. @ S. L.; _____ m. p. h. @ _____ ft. alt.; _____ m. p. h. @ _____ ft. alt.
Cruising speeds: Normal __192__ m. p. h.; economical __130__ m. p. h.; each at __13,000__ ft. altitude.
Climb: To __13,000__ ft. alt. in __10.2__ min.; rate _____ ft./min. at _____ ft. altitude.
Service ceilings: Normal load __27,000__ ft.; max. bomb/fuel load _____ ft.; min. fuel/no bombs __30,000__ ft.
Fuel: { U. S. gal.: Normal __136__ ; max. _____   Take-off, in calm air _____ ft.
       { Imp. gal.: Normal __113__ ; max. _____   Take-off, over 50 ft. obstacle _____ ft.

RANGES

Speeds	With Normal Fuel/Bomb Load __135__ U. S. gal. and __220__ lb. bombs	With Max. Bomb Load and _____ U. S. gal.	With Max. Fuel Load and _____ lb. Bombs
Economical cruising speed	● __130 mph – 540__ miles	_____ miles	_____ miles
Normal cruising speed	● __192 mph – 530__ miles	_____ miles	_____ miles
Maximum continuous speed	_____ miles	_____ miles	_____ miles
* Typical tactical speeds	_____ miles	_____ miles	_____ miles

*Ref.: p. 4. Para. 2.

POWER PLANT

                          1,000   2,300   2,500
No. engines __1__ , rated __940__ hp., each at __13,000__ ft. alt., with __2,500__ r. p. m. and __43.35__ in. Hg.

Description __Bramo "Fafnir" 323, 9-cylinder, air-cooled radial__

Specifications		Supercharger		Propeller		Fuel	
Bore __6.06__ in.	Dry Wgt. __1,320__ lbs.	No. Speeds __2__		Mfr. __V.D.M.__		Rating __87__ octane	
Stroke __6.3__ in.	Red. Gear __.621__	No. Stages _____		No. Blades __3__		Inlet System:	
Displ. __1,636__ cu. in.	Eng. Diam. __55.5__ in.	Ratios __9.6 : 12.4__		Diam. _____ ft., _____ in.		__Direct injection__	
Comp. Ratio __6.23__	Eng. Length __67.5__ in.	Impeller Diam. __9.92__ in.		Pitch Control _____			

ARMAMENT

(F—fixed. M—free.)

For'd fuselage __1/2x7.9mm (F)__
__500__ rpg.
__Port side of rear of cockpit firing aft, 1x7.9mm__
Through hub _____ (F)
Dorsal __2x7.9mm (M)__
Lateral __about 1,125 rpg.__
Ventral _____
Tail _____

BOMB/FREIGHT LOAD

Normal load __100__ kg., __220__ lb.
Max. load __280__ kg., __620__ lb.
Typical stowage
__10x22 lbs.__
_____
Alternate stowage
__8x22 + 4 x 110 lbs or 2x110 + 16x22 lbs.__
Freight _____ lb.
Troops _____

ARMOR

Frontal _____
Windshield _____
Pilot's seat __8mm__
_____
Dorsal _____
Lateral _____
Ventral _____
Bulkhead __8mm protects rear gunner__
Engine _____

SPECIFICATIONS

Materials __Metal, stressed skin; fabric and metal covering__

Span __47'-7"__   Length __35'-8"__   Height __12'-4"__   Gross wing area __341 sq. ft.__ Tail span _____

Weights: Landing __6,300__ lb.; normal load __7,250__ lb.; max. load _____ lb.

ADDITIONAL TECHNICAL DATA

Glider towing hook sometimes is fitted. Camera can be installed behind observer. Stowage
for hand camera in cockpit. Provision is made for smoke screen apparatus. One version has
BMW 132 engine.

DESCRIPTION

Mfr._____ Crew_____

Duty_____

PERFORMANCE

Max. emergency speeds_____ m. p. h. @ S. L.; _____ m. p. h. @ _____ ft. alt.; _____ m. p. h. @ _____ ft.alt.

Max. continuous speeds_____ m. p. h. @ S. L.; _____ m. p. h. @ _____ ft. alt.; _____ m. p. h. @ _____ ft. alt.

Cruising speeds: Normal _____ m. p. h.; ____ economical _____ m. p. h.; ____ each at_____ ft. altitude.

Climb: To ____ ft. alt. in _____ min.; rate_____ ft./min. at_____ ft. altitude.

Service ceilings: Normal load_____ ft.; max. bomb/fuel load_____ ft.; min. fuel/no bombs_____ ft.

Fuel: { U. S. gal.: Normal _____ ; max. _____ Take-off, in calm air_____ ft.

{ Imp. gal.: Normal _____ ; max. _____ Take-off, over 50 ft. obstacle_____ ft.

RANGES

Speeds	With Normal Fuel/Bomb Load _____ U. S. gal. and _____ lb. bombs	With Max. Bomb Load and _____ U. S. gal.	With Max. Fuel Load and _____ lb. Bombs
Economical cruising speed	_____ miles	_____ miles	_____ miles
Normal cruising speed	_____ miles	_____ miles	_____ miles
Maximum continuous speed	_____ miles	_____ miles	_____ miles
*Typical tactical speeds	_____ miles	_____ miles	_____ miles

*Ref.: p. 4. Para. 2.

POWER PLANT

No. engines_____ , rated_____ hp., each at _____ ft. alt., with_____ r. p. m. and_____ in. Hg.

Description_____

Specifications		Supercharger	Propeller	Fuel
Bore_____ in.	Dry Wgt._____ lbs.	No. Speeds_____	Mfr._____	Rating_____ octane
Stroke_____ in.	Red. Gear_____ : ____	No. Stages_____	No. Blades_____	Inlet System:_____
Displ._____ cu. in.	Eng. Diam. _____ in.	Ratios _____	Diam.____ ft.,____ in. _____	
Comp. Ratio ____ : _____	Eng. Length _____ in.	Impeller Diam._____ in.	Pitch Control_____	

ARMAMENT | BOMB/FREIGHT LOAD | ARMOR

(F—fixed.   M—free.)

For'd fuselage_____

_____

For'd wings_____

Through hub _____

Dorsal_____

Lateral_____

Ventral_____

Tail_____

Normal load_____ kg., _____ lb.

Max. load_____ kg., _____ lb.

Typical stowage _____

_____

Alternate stowage_____

_____

_____

Freight _____ lb.

Troops _____

Frontal_____

Windshield_____

Pilot's seat _____

_____

Dorsal_____

Lateral_____

Ventral_____

Bulkhead_____

_____

Engine _____

SPECIFICATIONS

Materials_____

Span _____ Length _____ Height _____ Gross wing area_____ Tail span _____

Weights: Landing_____ lb.; normal load_____ lb.; max. load_____ lb.

ADDITIONAL TECHNICAL DATA

_____

_____

_____

_____

_____

_____

AR 232

DESCRIPTION

The Ar 232 is a new type German transport.

It is a twin-engine, high-wing monoplane. Tricycle landing gear is used; single nose wheel may be replaced or supplemented by a group of small wheels. Some form of boundary layer control is employed over the trailing edge of the flaps; "drooping" ailerons are fitted. Forward fuselage is broad and deep. Section narrows abruptly 11' aft of trailing edge. Twin fins and rudders are employed.

TWIN-ENGINE TRANSPORT

Mfr. **ARADO**   Crew **THREE OR FOUR**

Duty **TRANSPORT**

PERFORMANCE (EST.)

Max. emergency speeds **180-185** m. p. h. @ S. L.; **210** m. p. h. @ **18,000** ft. alt.; _____ m. p. h. @ _____ ft.alt.

Max. continuous speeds _____ m. p. h. @ S. L.; _____ m. p. h. @ _____ ft. alt.; _____ m. p. h. @ _____ ft. alt.

Cruising speeds: Normal _____ m. p. h.; economical _____ m. p. h.; _____ each at _____ ft. altitude.

Climb: To _____ ft. alt. in _____ min.; rate _____ ft./min. at _____ ft. altitude.

Service ceilings: Normal load _____ ft.; max. bomb/fuel load _____ ft.; min. fuel/no bombs _____ ft.

Fuel: { U. S. gal.: Normal **(est) 600** ; max. _____ Take-off, in calm air _____ ft.

Fuel: { Imp. gal.: Normal **(est) 497** ; max. _____ Take-off, over 50 ft. obstacle _____ ft.

RANGES

Speeds	With Normal Fuel/Bomb Load **600** U. S. gal. and _____ lb. bombs		With Max. Bomb Load and _____ U. S. gal.	With Max. Fuel Load and _____ lb. Bombs
Economical cruising speed	_____ miles		_____ miles	_____ miles
Normal cruising speed	**900 - 1000** miles		_____ miles	_____ miles
Maximum continuous speed	_____ miles		_____ miles	_____ miles
*Typical tactical speeds	_____ miles		_____ miles	_____ miles

*Ref.: p. 4. Para. 2.

POWER PLANT

No. engines **2**, rated **1595 / 1495** hp., each at **17,750** ft. alt., with **4,000 / 2900 / 2900** r. p. m. and **38.14** in. Hg.

Description **Possibly BMW 801 A or L, 14 cylinder, twin-row, air-cooled radial.**

Specifications	Supercharger	Propeller	Fuel
Bore **6.14** in. Dry Wgt. **2960** lbs.	No. Speeds **2**	Mfr. _____	Rating **87** octane
Stroke **6.14** in. Red. Gear **.541**	No. Stages _____	No. Blades **3**	Inlet System: **Direct injection**
Displ. **2550** cu. in. Eng. Diam. **52** in.	Ratios **5.07; 7.47**	Diam. _____ ft., _____ in.	
Comp. Ratio **6.5** Eng. Length **58** in.	Impeller Diam. **13.25** in.	Pitch Control _____	

ARMAMENT

(F—fixed. M—free.)

For'd fuselage **Possibly 1 m.g.**

For'd wings _____

Through hub _____

Dorsal _____

Lateral **Possibly 4 m.g.'s**

Ventral _____

Tail _____

BOMB/FREIGHT LOAD

Normal load _____ kg., _____ lb.

Max. load _____ kg., _____ lb.

Typical stowage _____

Alternate stowage _____

Freight **(est) 9000** lb.

Troops _____

ARMOR

Frontal _____

Windshield _____

Pilot's seat _____

Dorsal _____

Lateral _____

Ventral _____

Bulkhead _____

Engine _____

SPECIFICATIONS

Materials **May be partly wooden.**

Span **(est) 104'** Length **(est) 77'** Height _____ Gross wing area _____ Tail span _____

Weights: Landing **(est) 35,800** lb.; normal load _____ lb.; max. load **(est) 49,300** lb.

ADDITIONAL TECHNICAL DATA

Floats or skis may be used. Deep section of fuselage is two-floor type; large double loading doors at back of deep section of fuselage, where it narrows abruptly.

B 71

DESCRIPTION

The B 71 is of the Soviet Union SB bomber design, built originally under license by Czechoslovakia and captured by Germany. The number of B 71 tugs in service is probably small.

It is a twin-engine, mid-wing monoplane. Wings, outboard of engine nacelles, have pronounced taper to rounded tips; root fillets are large. Flaps are fitted inboard and outboard of nacelles. There is a single fin and rudder; stabilizer is wire-braced. Pilot's cockpit is over leading edge; rear gunner's position is over trailing edge. Main wheels of landing gear retracts rearward into engine nacelles.

B 71

CAPTURED TWIN-ENGINE CZECH BOMBER, SOVIET SB TYPE

Mfr. ORIGINALLY CZECHOSLOVAKIA		Crew THREE	
Duty GLIDER AND TARGET TOWING			

PERFORMANCE

Max. emergency speeds __220__ m. p. h. @ S. L.; __260__ m. p. h. @ __12,000__ ft. alt.; _____ m. p. h. @ _____ ft.alt.

Max. continuous speeds _____ m. p. h. @ S. L.; _____ m. p. h. @ _____ ft. alt.; _____ m. p. h. @ _____ ft. alt.

Cruising speeds: Normal __215__ m. p. h.; economical __140__ m. p. h.; each at __12,000__ ft. altitude.

Climb: To __12,000__ ft. alt. in __6.7__ min.; rate _____ ft./min. at _____ ft. altitude.

Service ceilings: Normal load __30,000__ ft.; max. bomb/fuel load __29,300__ ft.; min. fuel/no bombs __32,800__ ft.

Fuel: U. S. gal.: Normal __225__ ; max. __424__ Take-off, in calm air _____ ft.

Imp. gal.: Normal __187__ ; max. __352__ Take-off, over 50 ft. obstacle _____ ft.

RANGES

Speeds	With Normal Fuel/Bomb Load __225__ U. S. gal. and __396__ lb. bombs	With Max. Bomb Load and _____ U. S. gal.	With Max. Fuel Load and __—__ lb. Bombs
Economical cruising speed	@ 140 mph – 605 miles	_____ miles	@145 mph – 1205 miles
Normal cruising speed	@ 215 mph – 490 miles	_____ miles	@215 mph – 970 miles
Maximum continuous speed	_____ miles	_____ miles	_____ miles
*Typical tactical speeds	_____ miles	_____ miles	_____ miles

*Ref.: p. 4. Para. 2.

POWER PLANT

No. engines __2__ , rated __860__ hp., each at __10,800__ ft. alt., with _____ r. p. m. and _____ in. Hg.

Description __Avia 12 Ydrs, 12 cylinder, liquid-cooled "V".__

Specifications	Supercharger	Propeller	Fuel
Bore _____ in. Dry Wgt. _____ lbs.	No. Speeds _____	Mfr. _____	Rating _____ octane
Stroke _____ in. Red. Gear _____ : _____	No. Stages _____	No. Blades __2 & 3__	Inlet System: _____
Displ. _____ cu. in. Eng. Diam. _____ in.	Ratios _____	Diam. _____ ft., _____ in.	
Comp. Ratio _____ : _____ Eng. Length _____ in.	Impeller Diam. _____ in.	Pitch Control _____	

ARMAMENT

(F—fixed. M—free.)

For'd fuselage __1/2 x 7.9mm (M)__

For'd wings _____

Through hub _____

Dorsal __Poss. 1/2 x 7.9mm (M)__

Lateral _____

Ventral __Poss. 1 x 7.9mm (M)__

Tail _____

BOMB/FREIGHT LOAD

Normal load _____ kg., _____ lb.

Max. load _____ kg., _____ lb.

Typical stowage _____

__Smoke bombs 396 lbs.__

Alternate stowage _____

Freight _____ lb.

Troops _____

ARMOR

Frontal _____

Windshield _____

Pilot's seat __Probably protected.__

Dorsal _____

Lateral _____

Ventral _____

Bulkhead _____

Engine _____

SPECIFICATIONS

Materials __Metal, stressed skin.__

Span __65'-11"__ Length __40'-7"__ Height _____ Gross wing area __615 sq. ft.__ Tail span _____

Weights: Landing __12,500__ lb.; normal load __14,500__ lb.; max. load _____ lb.

ADDITIONAL TECHNICAL DATA

Smoke bombs may be used for marking objective when aircraft is towing gliders. Sub-type "B", when

carrying 396 lbs. of smoke bombs, can only employ normal fuel load.

FW 58

DESCRIPTION

The FW 58 is a training aircraft that is used as a transport and ambulance.

It is a twin-engine, low-wing monoplane. Wing center section is braced by a single strut on each side of the fuselage. Leading edge tapers sharply outboard of the nacelles, tips rounded. Trailing edge is straight. Fuselage is of rectangular section. The stabilizer and elevators are braced; they are placed forward of the single fin and rudder. Landing gear retracts rearward into engine nacelles.

FW 58

"WEIHE"   TWIN-ENGINE TRANSPORT

Mfr. FOCKE-WULF   Crew THREE

Duty TRANSPORT. AMBULANCE. POSSIBLY BOMBING.

PERFORMANCE

Max. emergency speeds 143 m. p. h. @ S. L.; 141 m. p. h. @ 5,000 ft. alt.; _____ m. p. h. @ 10,000 ft.alt.

Max. continuous speeds _____ m. p. h. @ S. L.; _____ m. p. h. @ _____ ft. alt.; _____ m. p. h. @ _____ ft. alt.

Cruising speeds: Normal 123 m. p. h.; economical 75 m. p. h.; _____ each at sea level ft. altitude.

Climb: To 5,000 ft. alt. in 5.2 min.; rate _____ ft./min. at _____ ft. altitude.

Service ceilings: Normal load 20,500 ft.; max. bomb/fuel load 19,500 ft.; min. fuel/no bombs 23,200 ft.

Fuel: { U. S. gal.: Normal 122 ; max. 177 Take-off, in calm air _____ ft.

{ Imp. gal.: Normal 101 ; max. 147 Take-off, over 50 ft. obstacle _____ ft.

RANGES

Speeds	With Normal Fuel/Bomb Load 122 U. S. gal. and _____ lb. bombs	With Max. Bomb Load and _____ U. S. gal.	With Max. Fuel Load and _____ lb. Bombs
Economical cruising speed	@ 75 mph – 780 miles	_____ miles	@ 75 mph –1140 miles
Normal cruising speed	@ 123 mph – 505 miles	_____ miles	@ 122 mph –740 miles
Maximum continuous speed	_____ miles	_____ miles	_____ miles
*Typical tactical speeds	_____ miles	_____ miles	_____ miles

*Ref.: p. 4.   Para. 2.

POWER PLANT

No. engines 2 , rated 240 hp., each at S.L. ft. alt., with _____ r. p. m. and _____ in. Hg.

Description Argus As 10C, 8 cylinder, air-cooled inverted "V".

Specifications		Supercharger None	Propeller	Fuel
Bore 4.72 in.	Dry Wgt. 470 lbs.	No. Speeds _____	Mfr. _____	Rating 87 octane
Stroke 5.51 in.	Red. Gear None	No. Stages _____	No. Blades 2	Inlet System: _____
Displ. 771 cu. in.	Eng. Diam. 34.5 in.	Ratios _____	Diam. _ ft., _ in.	Carburetor
Comp. Ratio 5.9	Eng. Length 43.5 in.	Impeller Diam. _____ in.	Pitch Control _____	

ARMAMENT

(F—fixed.   M—free.)

For'd fuselage 1 x 7.9mm (M)

For'd wings _____

Through hub _____

Dorsal 1 x 7.9mm (M)

Lateral _____

Ventral _____

Tail _____

BOMB/FREIGHT LOAD

Normal load _____ kg., _____ lb.

Max. load _____ kg., _____ lb.

Typical stowage _____

_____

Alternate stowage _____

_____

Freight (est) 1,000 lb.

Troops (est) 8 men

ARMOR

None

Frontal _____

Windshield _____

Pilot's seat _____

Dorsal _____

Lateral _____

Ventral _____

Bulkhead _____

Engine _____

SPECIFICATIONS

Materials Metal, wood, fabric covering.

Span 68'-11"   Length 46'-4"   Height 13'-10"   Gross wing area 505 sq.ft.   Tail span _____

Weights: Landing 5,570 lb.;   normal load 6,350 lb.;   max. load _____ lb.

ADDITIONAL TECHNICAL DATA

Manually-operated mountings can be fitted in nose and dorsal position. Internal stowage for

light bomb load. Shape of fuselage may differ according to duty.

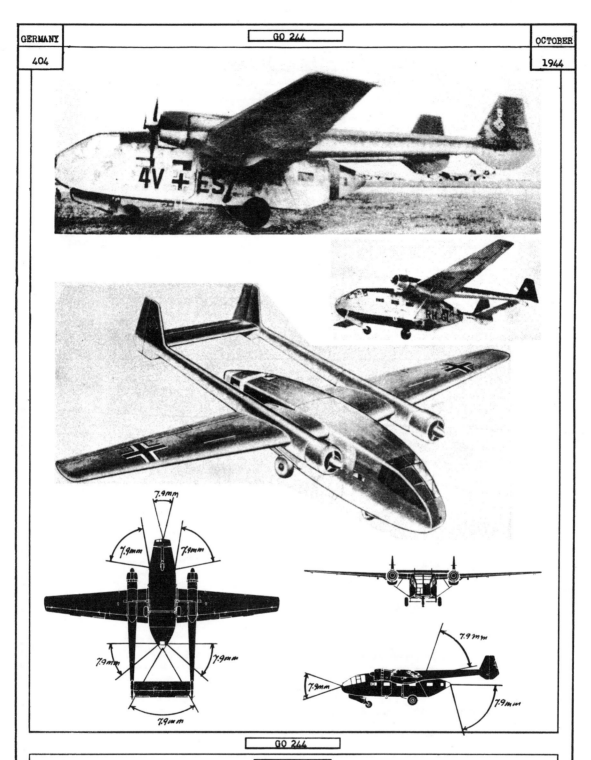

GO 244

DESCRIPTION

The Go 244 is a powered development of the Go 242 glider.

It is a twin-engine, high-wing, twin boom aircraft. The strut-braced wing tapers moderately to squared tips. Ailerons and flaps cover entire trailing edge. Lift spoilers are fitted on upper wing surfaces forward of outer portion of flaps. Nacelle is hinged at top aft of trailing edge for loading purposes. Forward upper part of nacelle is fitted with large windows. Tricycle landing gear is employed.

GO 244

TWIN-ENGINE POWERED VERSION OF GO 242 GLIDER

Mfr. __GOTHAER WAGGONFABRIK__   Crew __TWO__

Duty __TRANSPORT__

PERFORMANCE

Max. emergency speeds __146__ m. p. h. @ S. L.; __169__ m. p. h. @ __10,000__ ft. alt.; __157__ m. p. h. @ __5,000__ ft.alt.

Max. continuous speeds ____ m. p. h. @ S. L.; ____ m. p. h. @ ____ ft. alt.; ____ m. p. h. @ ____ ft. alt.

Cruising speeds: Normal __109__ m. p. h.; economical __100__ m. p. h.; ____ each at ____ __sea level__ ____ ft. altitude.

Climb: To __10,000__ ft. alt. in __20.2__ min.; rate ____ ft./min. at ____ ft. altitude.

Service ceilings: Normal load __19,000__ ft.; max. bomb/fuel load ____ ft.; min. fuel/no bombs __21,000__ ft.

Fuel: { U. S. gal.: Normal __(est) 217__ ; max. ____ Take-off, in calm air ____ ft.

{ Imp. gal.: Normal __(est) 180__ ; max. ____ Take-off, over 50 ft. obstacle ____ ft.

RANGES

Speeds	With Normal Fuel/Bomb Load __217__ U. S. gal. and __4400__ lb. bombs	With Max. Bomb Load and ____ U. S. gal.	With Max. Fuel Load and ____ lb. Bombs
Economical cruising speed	@ __100 mph - 375__ miles	____ miles	____ miles
Normal cruising speed	@ __109 mph - 360__ miles	____ miles	____ miles
Maximum continuous speed	____ miles	____ miles	____ miles
*Typical tactical speeds	____ miles	____ miles	____ miles

*Ref.: p. 4. Para. 2.

POWER PLANT

No. engines __2__ , rated __800__ hp., each at __8,000__ ft. alt., with ____ r. p. m. and ____ in. Hg.

Description __Gnome-Rhone 14M, 14 cylinder, twin-row, air-cooled radial.__

Specifications	Supercharger	Propeller	Fuel
Bore __4.80__ in. Dry Wgt. __920__ lbs.	No. Speeds __1__	Mfr. ____	Rating __87__ octane
Stroke __4.56__ in. Red. Gear __.765__	No. Stages ____	No. Blades __3__	Inlet System: ____
Displ. __1175__ cu. in. Eng. Diam. __39.0__ in.	Ratios __8.25__	Diam. ____ ft., ____ in.	Carburetor
Comp. Ratio __6.5__ Eng. Length ____ in.	Impeller Diam. ____ in.	Pitch Control ____	

ARMAMENT

(F—fixed. M—free.)

For'd fuselage __1/2 x 7.9mm (M)__

For'd wings ____

Through hub ____

Dorsal __1 x 7.9mm (M)__

Lateral __4 x 7.9mm__

Ventral ____

Tail __1 x 7.9mm (M)__

BOMB/FREIGHT LOAD

Normal load ____ kg., ____ lb.

Max. load ____ kg., ____ lb.

Typical stowage ____

Alternate stowage ____

Freight __4,400__ lb.

Troops __23 men__

ARMOR

Frontal __5 and 8mm__

Windshield ____

Pilot's seat __8mm sides__ __3mm bottom__

Dorsal ____

Lateral ____

Ventral ____

Bulkhead ____

Engine ____

SPECIFICATIONS

Materials __Wood and metal.__

Span __79'__   Length __52'-7"__   Height ____   Gross wing area __700 sq.ft.__   Tail span ____

Weights: Landing __15,900__ lb.; normal load __17,500__ lb.; max. load ____ lb.

ADDITIONAL TECHNICAL DATA

Armament fitted on manually-operated mountings. Cruising at 126 mph @10,000' range is 330 miles and at 116 mph, 340 miles.

HE 111Z

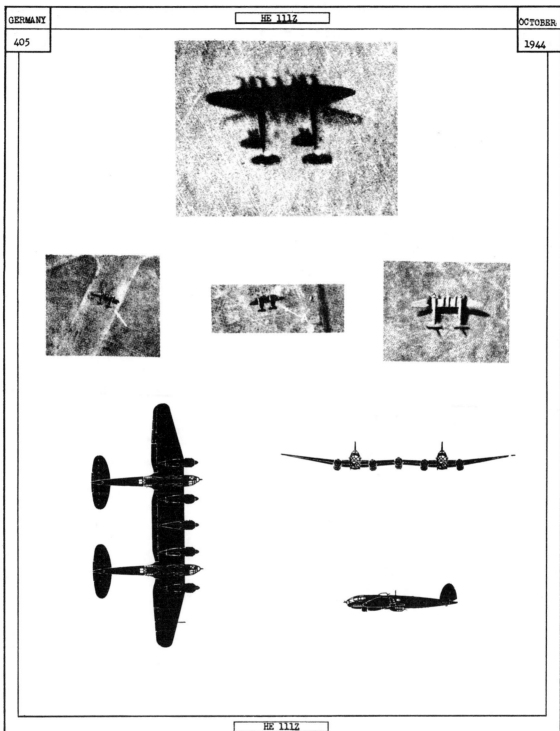

HE 111Z

DESCRIPTION

It is believed the primary function of the He 111Z is glider-towing.

It is a twin-fuselage, five-engined aircraft, apparently consisting of two He 111 fuselages, which are joined together by a specially-designed rectangular center section. Three engines are mounted in the leading edge of this center section, and one engine is placed in the inner section of each wing. The tail units are not joined together.

HE 111Z

TWIN–FUSELAGE GLIDER TUG/TRANSPORT

Mfr. __HEINKEL__   Crew __PROBABLY FIVE TO TEN__

Duty __GLIDER TUG. TRANSPORT__

PERFORMANCE   (EST.)

Max. emergency speeds _____ m. p. h. @ S. L.; __240/250__ m. p. h. @ __14,000__ ft. alt.; _____ m. p. h. @ _____ ft.alt
Max. continuous speeds _____ m. p. h. @ S. L.; _____ m. p. h. @ _____ ft. alt.; _____ m. p. h. @ _____ ft. alt.
Cruising speeds: Normal _____ m. p. h.; _____ economical _____ m. p. h.; _____ each at _____ ft. altitude.
Climb: To _____ ft. alt. in _____ min.; rate _____ ft./min. at _____ ft. altitude.
Service ceilings: Normal load _____ ft.; max. bomb/fuel load _____ ft.; min. fuel/no bombs _____ ft.
Fuel: { U. S. gal.: Normal __(est) 964__ ; max. __(est) 1808__   Take-off, in calm air _____ ft.
{ Imp. gal.: Normal __(est) 800__ ; max. __(est) 1500__   Take-off, over 50 ft. obstacle _____ ft.

RANGES

Speeds	With Normal Fuel/Bomb Load __964__ U. S. gal. and _____ lb. bombs	With Max. Bomb Load and _____ U. S. gal.	With Max. Fuel Load and _____ lb. Bombs
Economical cruising speed	__1,180__ miles	_____ miles	_____ miles
Normal cruising speed	_____ miles	_____ miles	_____ miles
Maximum continuous speed	_____ miles	_____ miles	_____ miles
*Typical tactical speeds	_____ miles	_____ miles	_____ miles

*Ref.: p. 4. Para. 2.

POWER PLANT

No. engines __5__ , rated { 1230 / 1075 } hp., each at __13,250__ ft. alt., with { 2600 } __2600__ r. p. m. and { 40.46 } __40.46__ in. Hg.

Description __Jumo 211F, 12 cylinder, liquid-cooled, inverted "V".__

Specifications		Supercharger	Propeller	Fuel
Bore __5.9__ in.	Dry Wgt. __1440__ lbs.	No. Speeds __2__	Mfr. __V.D.M.__	Rating __87__ octane
Stroke __6.5__ in.	Red. Gear __.545__	No. Stages _____	No. Blades __3__	Inlet System: __Direct__
Displ. __2130__ cu. in.	Eng. Diam. __32__ in.	Ratios __8.8; 12.4__	Diam. __ft., __in.	__injection__
Comp. Ratio __6.84__	Eng. Length __69__ in.	Impeller Diam. __8.91__ in.	Pitch Control _____	

ARMAMENT   BOMB/FREIGHT LOAD   ARMOR

(F—fixed. M—free.)   (EST.)   __Unknown__
See Additional Technical Data. Normal load _____ kg., _____ lb.   Frontal _____
For'd fuselage _____   Max. load _____ kg., _____ lb.   Windshield _____
                                    Typical stowage _____   Pilot's seat _____
For'd wings _____
                                                                          Dorsal _____
Through hub _____   Alternate stowage _____   Lateral _____
Dorsal _____   Ventral _____
Lateral _____   Bulkhead _____
Ventral _____   Freight __(est)__ __12,000__ lb.   _____
Tail _____   Troops __(est)__ __30 - 40 troops.__   Engine _____

SPECIFICATIONS

Materials __All-metal, stressed skin.__

Span __109'-8"__   Length __53'-8"__   Height __14'__   Gross wing area __(est) 1600 sq.ft.__ Tail span _____

Weights: Landing __39,580__ lb.; normal load __62,567__ lb.; max. load _____ lb.

ADDITIONAL TECHNICAL DATA

Ventral radiators between nacelles. Armament, if fitted, may be similar to He 111 bomber for each fuselage, as well as arcs of fire. DB 601 engines may replace Jumo 211s and in addition the central engine may sometimes be a BMW 801.

JU 52

DESCRIPTION

The Ju 52 is the standard freight and troop-carrying transport of the G.A.F. It is also used extensively as a parachute troop transport, and glider tug.

It is a three-engine, low-wing monoplane. Outer wing panels are attached by Junkers ball-joints. Junkers "double wing" is used, inner portions varying the chamber of the wing. Outer portions also "droop" but act differentially as ailerons. Fuselage is of rectangular section. There is a single fin and rudder. Landing gear is fixed. One engine is placed in the nose, other two in wings outboard of landing gear, forward of the leading edge. Outboard nacelles are "toed-out".

THREE-ENGINE TRANSPORT

Mfr. __JUNKERS__   Crew __THREE TO FOUR__

Duty __TRANSPORT. PARACHUTE DROPPING. GLIDER TUG. BOMBING.__

PERFORMANCE

Max. emergency speeds __165__ m. p. h. @ S. L.; _____ m. p. h. @ _____ ft. alt.; _____ m. p. h. @ _____ ft.alt.

Max. continuous speeds _____ m. p. h. @ S. L.; _____ m. p. h. @ _____ ft. alt.; _____ m. p. h. @ _____ ft. alt.

Cruising speeds: Normal __132__ m. p. h.; economical _____ m. p. h.; each at __sea level__ ft. altitude.

Climb: To _____ ft. alt. in _____ min.; rate _____ ft./min. at _____ ft. altitude.

Service ceilings: Normal load __16,000__ ft.; max. bomb/fuel load _____ ft.; min.*fuel/no bombs __20,000__ ft.

Fuel: { U. S. gal.: Normal __436__; max. __645__   Take-off, in calm air _____ ft.

{ Imp. gal.: Normal __362__; max. __535__   Take-off, over 50 ft. obstacle __1920__ ft.

RANGES

Speeds	With Normal Fuel/Bomb Load __436__ U. S. gal. and __5060__ lb. __fgt.__	With Max. Bomb Load and _____ U. S. gal.	With Max. Fuel Load and __4,000__ lb. Bombs
Economical cruising speed	_____ miles	_____ miles	_____ miles
Normal cruising speed	@ 132 mph – 530 miles	_____ miles	@132mph – 790 miles
Maximum continuous speed	_____ miles	_____ miles	_____ miles
*Typical tactical speeds	_____ miles	_____ miles	_____ miles

*Ref.: p. 4. Para. 2.

POWER PLANT

No. engines __3__, rated __660__ hp., each at __S.L.__ ft. alt., with _____ r. p. m. and _____ in. Hg.

Description __BMW 132A A/T, 9 cylinder, air-cooled radial.__

Specifications	Supercharger	Propeller	Fuel
Bore __6.12__ in. Dry Wgt. __1150__ lbs.	No. Speeds __1__	Mfr. _____	Rating __87__ octane
Stroke __6.37__ in. Red. Gear __.620__	No. Stages _____	No. Blades __2__	Inlet System: __Direct__
Displ. __1690__ cu. in. Eng. Diam. __54.5__ in.	Ratios __10.14__	Diam. __ ft., __ in.	__injection__
Comp. Ratio __6.9__ Eng. Length __49.5__ in.	Impeller Diam. __9.92__ in.	Pitch Control _____	

ARMAMENT

(F—fixed.   M—free.)

For'd fuselage __1 x 7.9mm (M)__

For'd wings _____

Through hub _____

Dorsal __1 x 7.9mm (M)__

Lateral __2 x 7.9mm (M)__

Ventral __1 x 7.9mm (M)__

Tail _____

BOMB/FREIGHT LOAD

Normal load _____ kg., _____ lb.

Max. load _____ kg., _____ lb.

Typical stowage _____

Alternate stowage _____

Freight __(est)__ __5060__ lb.

Troops __Up to 22 men__

ARMOR

__None__

Frontal _____

Windshield _____

Pilot's seat _____

Dorsal _____

Lateral _____

Ventral _____

Bulkhead _____

Engine _____

SPECIFICATIONS

Materials __Corrugated metal skin.__

Span __95'-11"__   Length __62'__   Height __14'-11"__   Gross wing area __1,190 sq.ft.__   Tail span _____

Weights: Landing __21,700__ lb.; normal load __23,100__ lb.; max. load _____ lb.

ADDITIONAL TECHNICAL DATA

Types g5e and g7e can be fitted with twin floats which have; max. speed of 155 mph @sea level; weight (normal load) of 24,200 lbs. finish 22,800 lbs; take-off over 50' obstacle of 3600 ft; service ceiling (at start) of 13,000 ft., at finish 15,000 ft; with 5060 lbs. of freight and 219 U.S. gal. of fuel and cruising at 120 mph @S.L. range is 230 miles; with 2,270 lbs. of freight and 645 U.S. gal. of fuel and cruising at 120 mph @S.L. range is 720 miles. Mine detonating ring, 47 ft. in diameter and consisting of 44 turns of aluminum rod inclosed in an oval light alloy fairing can be fitted. If BMW 132K engines, of 900 h.p. @9,000 ft., are used, performance would be increased slightly.

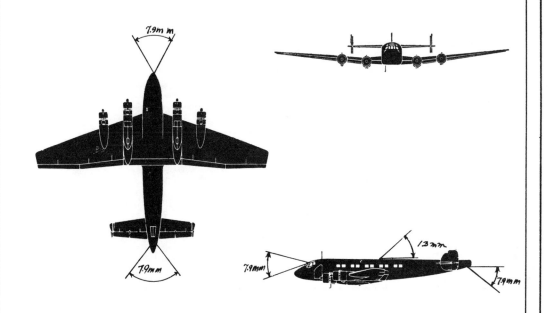

JU 90

DESCRIPTION

   The Ju 90 is one of the G.A.F.'s older military transports similar to the civil type bearing the same designation.
   It is a four-engine, low-wing monoplane. Wing leading edge is sharply-tapered; trailing edge is nearly straight; tips are "raked". Junkers "double wing" is employed, inner sections acting as flaps and outer sections as ailerons. There are twin fins and rudders. Landing gear retracts rearward into inboard engine nacelles. Later "straight-winged" type is generally similar but has rectangular center section and tapering outer panels with tips similar to the Ju 88A series.

JU 90

FOUR-ENGINE TRANSPORT

Mfr. __JUNKERS__ Crew __PROBABLY FIVE__

Duty __TRANSPORT. GLIDER TUG.__

PERFORMANCE

Max. emergency speeds _____ m. p. h. @ S. L.; __218__ m. p. h. @ __3500__ ft. alt.; _____ m. p. h. @ _____ ft.alt.
Max. continuous speeds _____ m. p. h. @ S. L.; _____ m. p. h. @ _____ ft. alt.; _____ m. p. h. @ _____ ft. alt.
Cruising speeds: Normal __178__ m. p. h.; economical __155__ m. p. h.; each at __5,000__ ft. altitude.
Climb: To __5,000__ ft. alt. in __6.5__ min.; rate _____ ft./min. at _____ ft. altitude.
Service ceilings: Normal load __15,000__ ft.; max. bomb/fuel load __13,500__ ft.; min. fuel/no bombs __18,000__ ft.
Fuel: { U. S. gal.: Normal __904__ ; max. __1663__ Take-off, in calm air _____ ft.
{ Imp. gal.: Normal __750__ ; max. __1380__ Take-off, over 50 ft. obstacle _____ ft.

RANGES

Speeds	With Normal Fuel/Bomb Load __844__ U. S. gal. and __9,000__ lb. Fgt.	With Max. Bomb Load and _____ U. S. gal.	With Max. Fuel Load and __5,000__ lb. Fgt.
Economical cruising speed	@ 155 mph – 810 miles	_____ miles	@160 mph – 1630 miles
Normal cruising speed	@ 178 mph – 785 miles	_____ miles	@177 mph – 1610 miles
Maximum continuous speed	_____ miles	_____ miles	_____ miles
*Typical tactical speeds	_____ miles	_____ miles	_____ miles

*Ref.: p. 4. Para. 2.

POWER PLANT

No. engines __4__ , rated __830__ hp, each at __3,600__ ft. alt., with _____ r. p. m. and _____ in. Hg.

Description __BMW 132H, 9 cylinder, air-cooled radial.__

Specifications		Supercharger	Propeller	Fuel
Bore __6.12__ in.	Dry Wgt. __1150__ lbs.	No. Speeds __1__	Mfr. __V.D.M./Junkers__	Rating __87__ octane
Stroke __6.37__ in.	Red. Gear __.620__	No. Stages _____	No. Blades __3__	Inlet System: __Direct__
Displ. __1690__ cu. in.	Eng. Diam. __54.5__ in.	Ratios __10.14__	Diam. __ ft., __ in.	__injection__
Comp. Ratio __6.9__	Eng. Length __49.5__ in.	Impeller Diam. __9.92__ in.	Pitch Control _____	

ARMAMENT

(F—fixed.   M—free.)

For'd fuselage __1 x 7.9mm (M)__

For'd wings _____

Through hub _____
Dorsal __1 x 13mm (M)__
Lateral _____
Ventral __Occ. 1 x 7.9mm (F)__
Tail _____

BOMB/FREIGHT LOAD

Normal load _____ kg., _____ lb.
Max. load __3500__ kg., __7700__ lb.
Typical stowage _____
__8 x 550 + 30 x 110 lbs.__

Alternate stowage _____

Freight __(normal)__ __9,000__ lb.
Troops __Up to 70 men__

ARMOR

Frontal _____
Windshield _____
Pilot's seat __Possibly protected.__

Dorsal _____
Lateral _____
Ventral _____
Bulkhead _____

Engine _____

SPECIFICATIONS

Materials __Metal, stressed skin.__

Span __115'__ Length __86'-2"__ Height (est) __21'__ Gross wing area __1980 sq.ft.__ Tail span _____

Weights: Landing __45,700__ lb.; normal load __51,000__ lb.; max. load __54,000__ lb.

ADDITIONAL TECHNICAL DATA

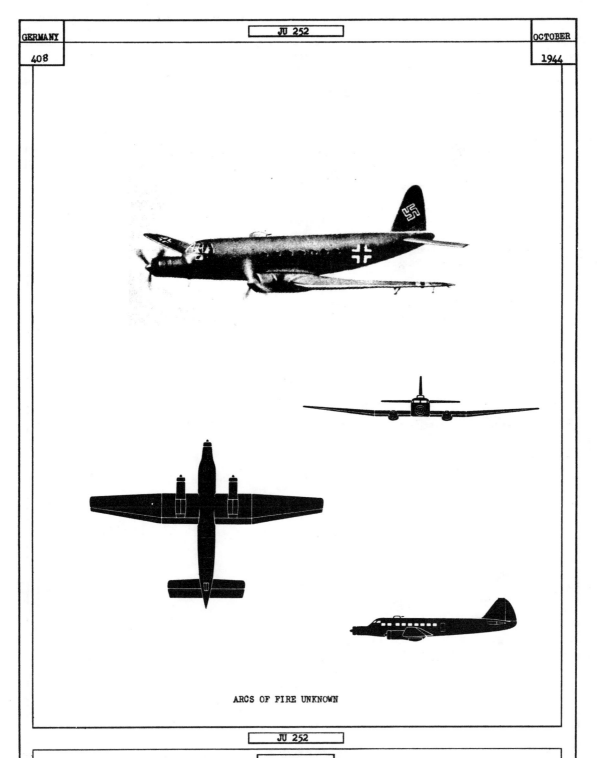

ARCS OF FIRE UNKNOWN

JU 252

DESCRIPTION

    The Ju 252 is a transport developed from the Ju 52.

    It is a three-engine, low-wing monoplane. Wing center section is rectangular; outer panels taper, more so on trailing than leading edges. Tips are blunt. Fuselage is broad and deep with a "snout-shaped" long nose which drops down sharply to the center engine. There is a single fin and rudder. Landing gear retracts. It is reported that a retractable loading ramp is built into the bottom of the fuselage as on the Ju 290.

JU 252

THREE-ENGINE TRANSPORT

Mfr. __JUNKERS__   Crew __SIX__

Duty __TRANSPORT. POSSIBLY BOMBING.__

PERFORMANCE

Max. emergency speeds __200__ m. p. h. @ S. L.; __235__ m. p. h. @ __18,500__ ft. alt.; _____ m. p. h. @ _____ ft.alt.

Max. continuous speeds _____ m. p. h. @ S. L.; _____ m. p. h. @ _____ ft. alt.; _____ m. p. h. @ _____ ft. alt.

Cruising speeds: Normal __200__ m. p. h.; economical _____ m. p. h.; each at _____ ft. altitude.

Climb: To _____ ft. alt. in _____ min.; rate _____ ft./min. at _____ ft. altitude.

Service ceilings: Normal load __(est) 26,000__ ft.; max. bomb/fuel load _____ ft.; min. fuel/no bombs _____ ft.

Fuel: U. S. gal.: Normal __(est) 1,446__ ; max. __(est) 2,410__ Take-off, in calm air _____ ft.

Imp. gal.: Normal __(est) 1,200__ ; max. __2,000__ Take-off, over 50 ft. obstacle _____ ft.

RANGES

Speeds	With Normal Fuel/Bomb Load U. S. gal. and ____ lb. bombs		With Max. Bomb Load and ____ U. S. gal.	With Max. Fuel Load and ____ lb. Bombs
Economical cruising speed	_____	miles	_____ miles	_____ miles
Normal cruising speed	_____	miles	_____ miles	_____ miles
Maximum continuous speed	_____	miles	_____ miles	_____ miles
*Typical tactical speeds	_____	miles	_____ miles	_____ miles

*Ref.: p. 4. Para. 2.

POWER PLANT

No. engines __3__ , rated __1755 / 1530__ hp, each at __3,250 / 20,000__ ft. alt., with _____ r. p. m. and _____ in. Hg.

Description __BMW 801, 14 cylinder, twin-row, air-cooled, fan-assisted radial.__

Specifications	Supercharger	Propeller	Fuel
Bore __6.14__ in. Dry Wgt. __2960__ lbs.	No. Speeds __2__	Mfr. __V.D.M.__	Rating __100__ octane
Stroke __6.14__ in. Red. Gear __.541__	No. Stages _____	No. Blades __3__	Inlet System: __Direct__
Displ. __2550__ cu. in. Eng. Diam. __52__ in.	Ratios __5.31; 8.32__	Diam. ____ ft., ____ in.	__injection__
Comp. Ratio __7.1__ Eng. Length _____ in.	Impeller Diam. __13.25__ in.	Pitch Control _____	

ARMAMENT (EST.)

(F—fixed. M—free.)

For'd fuselage _____

_____

For'd wings _____

Through hub

Dorsal __1 x 13/20mm (M)__

Lateral __? x 7.9mm (M)__

Ventral __1 x 13mm (M)__

Tail __1 x 13/30mm (M)__

BOMB/FREIGHT LOAD

Normal load _____ kg., _____ lb.

Max. load _____ kg., _____ lb.

Typical stowage _____

_____

Alternate stowage _____

_____

Freight __(est)__ __12,000__ lb.

Troops __35 men__

ARMOR

Frontal _____

Windshield _____

Pilot's seat __Probably protected.__

Dorsal _____

Lateral _____

Ventral _____

Bulkhead _____

_____

Engine _____

SPECIFICATIONS

Materials __Metal, stressed skin, plywood.__

Span __(est) 111'__   Length __(est) 77'__   Height __(est) 15'__   Gross wing area __1600 sq. ft.__   Tail span __37'__

Weights: Landing _____ lb.; normal load __(est) 45,000__ lb.; max. load _____ lb.

ADDITIONAL TECHNICAL DATA

Reports indicate up to six gun positions. It is known that there is a dorsal turret, probably hydraulically-operated, just forward of wing leading edge. Rear lower fuselage drops to form loading ramp as on Ju 290. May be fitted with Jumo 211 engines.

JU 290

The Ju 290 was developed from the Ju 90 and is currently-operational.

It is a four-engine, low-wing monoplane. Wing center section is rectangular; outer panels taper to blunt tips. Fuselage is of square section with rounded corners. Pilot's cockpit is placed well forward in nose. Twin fins and rudders of either oval or angular shape are placed at extremities of stabilizer that has some dihedral. Landing gear has double wheels and retracts hydraulically rearward into inboard nacelles; tailwheel is fully retractable.

JU 290

FOUR-ENGINE TRANSPORT

Mfr. __JUNKERS_____ Crew __PROBABLY FOUR TO SEVEN__

Duty __TRANSPORT. POSSIBLY GLIDER TOWING OR BOMBING._____

PERFORMANCE

Max. emergency speeds __209__ m. p. h. @ S. L.; __243__ m. p. h. @ __18,000__ ft. alt.; __212__ m. p. h. @ __8,000__ ft. alt.
Max. continuous speeds_____ m. p. h. @ S. L.; _____ m. p. h. @ _____ ft. alt.; _____ m. p. h. @ _____ ft. alt.
Cruising speeds: Normal __203__ m. p. h.; economical __191__ m. p. h.; each at __18,000__ ft. altitude.
Climb: To __18,000__ ft. alt. in __43.5__ min.; rate _____ ft./min. at _____ ft. altitude.
Service ceilings: Normal load __19,000__ ft.; max. bomb/fuel load _____ ft.; min. fuel/no bombs __23,000__ ft.
Fuel: { U. S. gal.: Normal __1,909__ ; max. __(est) 3319__ Take-off, in calm air _____ ft.
Fuel: { Imp. gal.: Normal __1,584__ ; max. __(est) 2754__ Take-off, over 50 ft. obstacle _____ ft.

RANGES

Speeds	With Normal Fuel/Bomb Load __1909__ U. S. gal. and __19,000__ lb. fgt.	With Max. Bomb Load and _____ U. S. gal.	With Max. Fuel Load and __10,000__ lb. Bombs
Economical cruising speed	@ 191 mph – 1030 miles	_____ miles	@186 mph –2010 miles
Normal cruising speed	@ 203 mph – 990 miles	_____ miles	@208 mph ~1880 miles
Maximum continuous speed	_____ miles	_____ miles	_____ miles
*Typical tactical speeds	_____ miles	_____ miles	_____ miles

*Ref.: p. 4. Para. 2.

POWER PLANT

No. engines __4__ , rated __1500__ hp., each at __18,000__ ft. alt., with _____ r. p. m. and _____ in. Hg.

Description __BMW 801 L-2, 14 cylinder, twin-row, air-cooled radial.__

Specifications	Supercharger	Propeller	Fuel
Bore __6.14__ in. Dry Wgt. __2960__ lbs.	No. Speeds __2__	Mfr. __V.D.M.__	Rating __100__ octane
Stroke __6.14__ in. Red. Gear __.541__	No. Stages _____	No. Blades __3__	Inlet System: __Direct__
Displ. __2550__ cu. in. Eng. Diam. __52__ in.	Ratios __5.31; 8.32__	Diam. __ ft. __ in.	__injection__
Comp. Ratio __7.1__ Eng. Length _____ in.	Impeller Diam. _____ in.	Pitch Control _____	

ARMAMENT / BOMB/FREIGHT LOAD / ARMOR

ARMAMENT

(F—fixed. M—free.)
(All Free)
For'd fuselage __Poss. 1 x 20mm__
_____
For'd wings_____
_____
Through hub_____
Dorsal __1 x 15/20mm, fore & aft__
Lateral __4/6 x 7.9 or 2 x 13mm__
Ventral __(rear) 1 x 13;(fwd)1x20mm__
Tail __1 x 20mm (M)__

BOMB/FREIGHT LOAD

Normal load_____ kg., _____ lb.
Max. load_____ kg., _____ lb.
Typical stowage_____
_____
Alternate stowage_____ __Freight space approximately 3190 cu. ft.__
Freight __19,000__ lb.
Troops __Up to 90 men.__

ARMOR

Frontal_____
Windshield_____
Pilot's seat __Probably protected.__
_____
Dorsal_____
Lateral_____
Ventral_____
Bulkhead_____
_____
Engine _____

SPECIFICATIONS

Materials __Metal, stressed skin.__

Span __138'__ Length __92'-10"__ Height __18'__ Gross wing area __2,210 sq.ft.__ Tail span _____

Weights: Landing __68,000__ lb.; normal load __90,000__ lb.; max. load _____ lb.

ADDITIONAL TECHNICAL DATA

Retractable loading ramp 16'-2" long by 7'-8" wide built into bottom of rear fuselage. It is mechanically-operated and acts as a jack which lifts tail of the aircraft clear of the ground to facilitate loading. One dorsal turret is hydraulically-operated; ventral gunner's position is under port side of fuselage forward of wing; tail gun mounting appears to be manually-operated. Leading edges wing and stabilizer de-iced by hot air; propellers de-iced by fluid; cabin is heated. May be converted into heavy bomber with 2 x 20mm in dorsal turrets, 2 x 13mm in lateral positions and twin 7.9mm in tail.

ME 323

DESCRIPTION

The Me 323 is the powered version of the Me 321 "Gigant" glider, and was used extensively in the North African campaign. Due to its large load-carrying capacity, it probably will continue to form an important part of G.A.F. transport aircraft.

It is a six-engine, high-wing monoplane. Strut-braced wing has moderate taper to blunt tips. Flaps are hydraulically-operated. Fuselage is of rectangular section. Nose of fuselage splits vertically to form two doors which swing open sideways, making an aperture 10'-10" high x 9'-3" wide. Pilot's cockpit is on top of fuselage, forward of leading edge. There is a single fin and rudder and strut-braced stabilizer. The whole tail unit moves when stabilizer incidence is changed. Landing gear has five wheels on each side of the fuselage inclosed in long fairings.

ME 323

SIX-ENGINE POWERED VERSION OF ME 321 GLIDER

Mfr. MESSERSCHMITT   Crew PROBABLY EIGHT TO TEN

Duty TRANSPORT

PERFORMANCE

Max. emergency speeds 163 m. p. h. @ S. L.; 194 m. p. h. @ 13,000 ft. alt.; 183 m. p. h. @ 20,000 ft.alt.

Max. continuous speeds _____ m. p. h. @ S. L.; _____ m. p. h. @ _____ ft. alt.; _____ m. p. h. @ _____ ft. alt.

Cruising speeds: Normal 163 m. p. h.; economical 129 m. p. h.; each at _____ ft. altitude.

Climb: To 13,000 ft. alt. in 18 min.; rate _____ ft./min. at _____ ft. altitude.

Service ceilings: Normal load 23,000 ft.; max. bomb/fuel load 20,300 ft.; min. fuel/no bombs 25,000 ft.

Fuel: { U. S. gal.: Normal 1,424 ; max. _____ Take-off, in calm air _____ ft.

{ Imp. gal.: Normal 1,182 ; max. _____ Take-off, over 50 ft. obstacle _____ ft.

RANGES

Speeds	With Normal Fuel/Bomb Load 1424 U. S. gal. and 26,900 lb. fgt.	With Max. Fgt. Load and 478 U. S. gal.	With Max. Fuel Load and _____ lb. Bombs
Economical cruising speed	@ 129 mph - 720 miles	@ 139mph -140 miles	_____ miles
Normal cruising speed	@ 163 mph - 640 miles	_____ miles	_____ miles
Maximum continuous speed	_____ miles	_____ miles	_____ miles
*Typical tactical speeds	_____ miles	_____ miles	_____ miles

*Ref.: p. 4. Para. 2.

POWER PLANT

No. engines 6 , rated 965 hp., each at 13,100 ft. alt., with _____ r. p. m. and 36.3 in. Hg.

Description Gnôme-Rhône 14N 48/49, 14 cylinder, twin-row, air-cooled radial.

Specifications		Supercharger		Propeller		Fuel	
Bore 5.75 in.	Dry Wgt. 1370 lbs.	No. Speeds 1		Mfr. _____		Rating _____ octane	
Stroke 6.5 in.	Red. Gear .666	No. Stages _____		No. Blades 2 or 3		Inlet System:	
Displ. 2370 cu. in.	Eng. Diam. 50.07 in.	Ratios 8.94		Diam. ___ ft., ___ in.		Carburetor	
Comp. Ratio 6.1	Eng. Length 66.1 in.	Impeller Diam. 11.58 in.		Pitch Control _____			

ARMAMENT

(F—fixed. M—free.)

(All Free)

For'd fuselage 2 x 7.9mm - upper

2 x 7.9mm - lower

Dorsal 4 x 7.9mm - fwd.

2 x 7.9mm - rear

Through hub _____

Lateral 6 x 7.9mm

Ventral 2 x 7.9mm aft.

Tail _____

BOMB/FREIGHT LOAD

Normal load _____ kg., _____ lb.

Max. load _____ kg., _____ lb.

Typical stowage _____

Alternate stowage _____

Freight Normal, 26,900; overload, 44,800 lb.

Troops 60 to 100 men.

ARMOR

Frontal _____

Windshield 2½" bulletproof glass

Pilot's seat 6-15mm armored box houses both pilots.

Dorsal _____

Lateral 8-10 back & head for engineers.

Ventral _____

Bulkhead _____

Engine _____

SPECIFICATIONS

Materials Metal, wood, steel tubing, fabric.

Span 181'   Length 93'-4"   Height 27'-6"   Gross wing area 3,270 sq.ft.   Tail span _____

Weights: Landing 74,500 lb.; normal load 85,000 lb.; max. load 95,000 lb.

ADDITIONAL TECHNICAL DATA

Two flight engineers, who control engines, are carried in cabins in the leading edge between inner and center engines, entered through cat walks in wing; cabins have sliding roofs; only flight controls in pilot's cockpit. 18 gun positions are available, but are not all used simultaneously. Provision for four rockets for assisted take-off placed under each wing. Fuel tanks in wing roots and over fuselage in wing. Main loading space of about 2,000 cu.ft. capacity capable of holding a 3-ton truck or light tank. A secondary loading space of about 1410 cu.ft. capacity can be obtained by suspending a floor from the main top longitudinal members. A pump is fitted in fuselage for re-fueling in flight from barrels carried as cargo. Guns of 13mm calibre may replace the 7.9mm guns.

DESCRIPTION

[ ]

Mfr._____ Crew_____

Duty_____

PERFORMANCE

Max. emergency speeds_____ m. p. h. @ S. L.;_____ m. p. h. @_____ ft. alt.;_____ m. p. h. @_____ ft.alt.
Max. continuous speeds_____ m. p. h. @ S. L.;_____ m. p. h. @_____ ft. alt.;_____ m. p. h. @_____ ft. alt.
Cruising speeds: Normal_____ m. p. h.;____ economical_____ m. p. h.;____ each at_____ ft. altitude.
Climb: To_____ ft. alt. in_____ min.; rate_____ ft./min. at_____ ft. altitude.
Service ceilings: Normal load_____ ft.; max. bomb/fuel load_____ ft.; min. fuel/no bombs_____ ft.
Fuel: {U. S. gal.: Normal_____ ; max._____ Take-off, in calm air_____ ft.
{Imp. gal.: Normal_____ ; max._____ Take-off, over 50 ft. obstacle_____ ft.

RANGES

Speeds	With Normal Fuel/Bomb Load_____ U. S. gal. and_____ lb. bombs	With Max. Bomb Load and_____ U. S. gal.	With Max. Fuel Load and_____ lb. Bombs
Economical cruising speed	_____ miles	_____ miles	_____ miles
Normal cruising speed	_____ miles	_____ miles	_____ miles
Maximum continuous speed	_____ miles	_____ miles	_____ miles
*Typical tactical speeds	_____ miles	_____ miles	_____ miles

*Ref.: p. 4. Para. 2.

POWER PLANT

No. engines_____ , rated_____ hp., each at_____ ft. alt., with_____ r. p. m. and_____ in. Hg.

Description_____

Specifications	Supercharger	Propeller	Fuel
Bore_____ in. Dry Wgt._____ lbs.	No. Speeds_____	Mfr._____	Rating_____ octane
Stroke_____ in. Red. Gear____ .____	No. Stages_____	No. Blades_____	Inlet System:_____
Displ._____ cu. in. Eng. Diam._____ in.	Ratios_____	Diam.____ ft., ____ in._____	
Comp. Ratio_____ Eng. Length____ ____ in.	Impeller Diam._____ in.	Pitch Control_____	

ARMAMENT   BOMB/FREIGHT LOAD   ARMOR

(F—fixed. M—free.)

For'd fuselage_____
_____
For'd wings_____
Through hub_____
Dorsal_____
Lateral_____
Ventral_____
Tail_____

Normal load_____ kg.,_____ lb.
Max. load_____ kg.,_____ lb.
Typical stowage_____
_____
Alternate stowage_____
_____
Freight_____ lb.
Troops_____

Frontal_____
Windshield_____
Pilot's seat_____
_____
Dorsal_____
Lateral_____
Ventral_____
Bulkhead_____
_____
Engine_____

SPECIFICATIONS

Materials_____

Span_____ Length_____ Height_____ Gross wing area_____ Tail span_____

Weights: Landing_____ lb.; normal load_____ lb.; max. load_____ lb.

ADDITIONAL TECHNICAL DATA

_____
_____
_____
_____
_____

AR 196

DESCRIPTION

The Ar 196 is a standard fighter-reconnaissance aircraft of the G.A.F. It is designed for catapult operation from warships and from shore bases. Intended primarily for reconnaissance as "the eyes of the Fleet", it also is used for attacks on long range reconnaissance aircraft.

It is a single-engine, low-wing monoplane with either a single float and stabilising wing floats or twin floats. Wings are designed to fold; they have straight leading and trailing edges and a slight taper. Tips are rounded. Fuselage is of oval structure. The single fin and rudder is set well forward in relation to the stabiliser. Cockpit inclosure is transparent. Fuel is carried in floats which are of the single-step type and are attached to fuselage by tubular struts.

AR 196

SINGLE—ENGINE FLOATPLANE

Mfr. **ARADO**   Crew **TWO**

Duty **FIGHTING. RECONNAISSANCE. BOMBING.**

PERFORMANCE

Max. emergency speeds **195** m. p. h. @ S. L.; _____ m. p. h. @ _____ ft.alt.; _____ m. p. h. @ _____ ft.alt.
Max. continuous speeds _____ m. p. h. @ S. L.; _____ m. p. h. @ _____ ft. alt.; _____ m. p. h. @ _____ ft. alt.
Cruising speeds: Normal **175** m. p. h.; economical **120** m. p. h.; each at **6,000** ft. altitude.
Climb: To **6,000** ft. alt. in **4.5** min.; rate _____ ft./min. at _____ ft. altitude.
Service ceilings: Normal load **21,500** ft.; max. bomb/fuel load **17,500** ft.; min. fuel/no bombs **23,500** ft.
Fuel: { U. S. gal.: Normal **159** ; max. _____ Take-off, in calm air _____ ft.
{ Imp. gal.: Normal **132** ; max. _____ Take-off, over 50 ft. obstacle _____ ft.

RANGES

Speeds	With Normal Fuel/Bomb Load _____ U. S. gal. and _____ lb. bombs		With Max. Bomb Load and _____ **137** _____ U. S. gal.	With Max. Fuel Load and _____ lb. Bombs
Economical cruising speed	_____ miles		@**120 mph** — **540** miles	@**120 mph** — **600** miles
Normal cruising speed	_____ miles		@**175 mph** — **460** miles	@**175 mph** — **530** miles
Maximum continuous speed	_____ miles		_____ miles	_____ miles
*Typical tactical speeds	_____ miles		_____ miles	_____ miles

*Ref.: p. 4. Para. 2.

POWER PLANT

No. engines **1** , rated **920** hp., each at **S.L.** ft. alt., with **2550** r. p. m. and **37.57** in. Hg.

Description **BMW 132K, 9 cylinder, air-cooled radial.**

Specifications		Supercharger	Propeller	Fuel
Bore **6.12** in.	Dry Wgt. **1150** lbs.	No. Speeds **1**	Mfr. _____	Rating **87** octane
Stroke **6.37** in.	Red. Gear **.720**	No. Stages _____	No. Blades **2 or 3**	Inlet System: **Direct**
Displ. **1690** cu. in.	Eng. Diam. **54.5** in.	Ratios **7.0**	Diam. ___ ft., ___ in.	**injection.**
Comp. Ratio **6.9**	Eng. Length **49.5** in.	Impeller Diam. **9.92** in.	Pitch Control _____	

ARMAMENT

(F—fixed.   M—free.)

For'd fuselage **1 x 7.9mm (F)**

For'd wings **2 x 20mm (F)**

Through hub _____
Dorsal **Twin 7.9mm (M)**
Lateral _____
Ventral _____
Tail _____

BOMB/FREIGHT LOAD

Normal load _____ kg., _____ lb.
Max. load **100** kg., **220** lb.
Typical stowage
2 x 110 lbs.

Alternate stowage _____

Freight _____ lb.
Troops _____

ARMOR

Frontal _____
Windshield _____
Pilot's seat **Probably protected.**

Dorsal _____
Lateral _____
Ventral _____
Bulkhead _____

Engine _____

SPECIFICATIONS

Materials **Metal, stressed skin, fabric.**

Span **41'** Length **36'-1"** Height **13'** Gross wing area **307 sq.ft.** Tail span _____

Weights: Landing **5,500** lb.; normal load **6,600** lb.; max. load **6,800** lb.

ADDITIONAL TECHNICAL DATA

Oil cooler in leading edge on port wing. Bomb carriers under wing. Stressed for catapult launching. Although twin-float version is standard, single float model with wing lateral stabilizing floats exists. Maximum speed of pull-out from dive is 316 mph.

BV 138

DESCRIPTION

The BV 138 is one of the most important marine aircraft of the G.A.F.

It is a three-engine, high-wing monoplane with twin booms. Center section of wing is attached directly to the hull. The hull is short and of the single-step type with a shallow "V" bottom and straight sides. The center engine is placed in a nacelle above the center section; the outboard engines are in nacelles at the extremities of the center section. A stabilizing float is fitted under each wing on a single strut. The stabilizer is fitted between the booms, which terminate in the twin fins and rudders.

BV 138

THREE ENGINE FLYING BOAT

Mfr. **BLOHM & VOSS**   Crew **FIVE TO SIX**

Duty **RECONNAISSANCE. BOMBING. MINE-LAYING.**

PERFORMANCE

Max. emergency speeds **175** m. p. h. @ S. L.; _____ m. p. h. @ _____ ft. alt.; _____ m. p. h. @ _____ ft.alt.
Max. continuous speeds _____ m. p. h. @ S. L.; _____ m. p. h. @ _____ ft. alt.; _____ m. p. h. @ _____ ft. alt.
Cruising speeds: Normal **145** m. p. h.; economical **120** m. p. h.; each at **Sea level** ft. altitude.
Climb: To **10,000** ft. alt. in **14.6** min.; rate _____ ft./min. at _____ ft. altitude.
Service ceilings: Normal load **17,000** ft.; max. bomb/fuel load **10,000** ft.; min. fuel/no bombs **25,000** ft.
Fuel: { U. S. gal.: Normal **466** ; max. (est) **1452** Take-off, in calm air _____ ft.
{ Imp. gal.: Normal **387** ; max. (est) **1205** Take-off, over 50 ft. obstacle _____ ft.

RANGES

Speeds	With Normal Fuel/Bomb Load **466** U. S. gal. and **1,400** lb. bombs	With Max. Bomb Load and **1162** U. S. gal.	With Max. Fuel Load and **2,200** lb. Bombs
Economical cruising speed	@ 120 mph – 1,140 miles	@125mph –2,500 miles	@125mph–3,120 miles
Normal cruising speed	@ 145 mph – 990 miles	@140mph –2,200 miles	@140mph–2,760 miles
Maximum continuous speed	_____ miles	_____ miles	_____ miles
*Typical tactical speeds	_____ miles	_____ miles	_____ miles

*Ref.: p. 4. Para. 2.

POWER PLANT

No. engines **3** , rated **700** hp., each at **S.L.** ft. alt., with **2600 .** r. p. m. and _____ in. Hg.

Description **Jumo 205D, 6 cylinder, opposed piston, two stroke, liquid-cooled diesel.**

Specifications	Supercharger	Propeller	Fuel
Bore **4.13** in. Dry Wgt. **1257** lbs.	No. Speeds **1**	Mfr. _____	Rating **Fuel oil** octane
Stroke **6.3** in. Red. Gear **.724**	No. Stages _____	No. Blades **3 & 4**	Inlet System: **Direct**
Displ. **1014** cu. in. Eng. Diam. **23.6** in.	Ratios **8.9**	Diam. ___ ft., ___ in.	**injection**
Comp. Ratio **17 : 1** Eng. Length **80** in.	Impeller Diam. _____ in.	Pitch Control _____	

ARMAMENT

(F—fixed. M—free.)

For'd fuselage **1 x 15/20mm (M)**
For'd wings _____
Through hub _____
Dorsal **1 x 13mm (M)**
Lateral _____
Ventral _____
Tail **1 x 15/20mm (M)**

BOMB/FREIGHT LOAD

Normal load **300** kg., **660** lb.
Max. load **1820** kg., **4000** lb.
Typical stowage _____
        / **6 x 110 lbs.**
    4 x 330 lb. depth charges
Alternate stowage **2 x 550 lbs.**
(est) Torpedoes or mines.
2 x 1540/1980 lbs.
Freight _____ lb.
Troops **Up to eight men**

ARMOR

Frontal _____
Windshield _____
Pilot's seat **Probably protected.**

Dorsal _____
Lateral _____
Ventral _____
Bulkhead _____
Engine _____

SPECIFICATIONS

Materials **Metal, stressed skin.**

Span **88'-7"** Length **62'-4"** Height **21'-8"** Gross wing area **1,205 sq.ft.** Tail span _____

Weights: Landing **26,500** lb.; normal load **30,800** lb.; max. load **38,500** lb.

ADDITIONAL TECHNICAL DATA

Radiators underslung. Turrets are hydraulically-operated. External bomb carriers between outboard nacelles and hull. Stressed for catapulting. Take-off rockets reported.

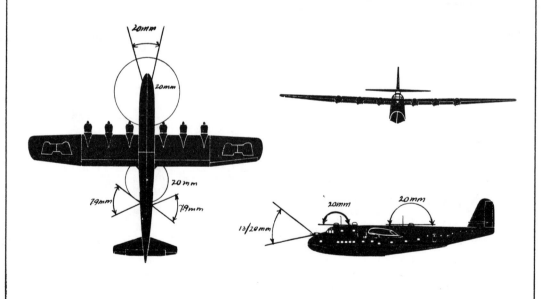

BV 222

DESCRIPTION

The BV 222 is probably the largest aircraft, excluding gliders, produced for the G.A.F. since the outbreak of the war.

It is a six-engine, high-wing monoplane. Inner wing sections are nearly straight; outer panels taper moderately to blunt tips. The two-step hull is long and deep with straight sides, and has at least 2 decks. Pilot's cockpit is forward of wing. The wing-stabilizing floats divide down the center, each portion retracting spanwise into the wing. The stabilizer is set part-way up on the tall, single fin and rudder.

| BV 222 |

SIX-ENGINE FLYING BOAT

Mfr. __BLOHM & VOSS__   Crew __PROBABLY TEN__

Duty __TRANSPORT__

PERFORMANCE (EST.)

Max. emergency speeds _____ m. p. h. @ S. L.; __200/240__ m. p. h. @ __15/17000__ ft. alt.; _____ m. p. h. @ _____ ft.alt.

Max. continuous speeds _____ m. p. h. @ S. L.; _____ m. p. h. @ _____ ft. alt.; _____ m. p. h. @ _____ ft. alt.

Cruising speeds: Normal __150__ m. p. h.; _____ economical _____ m. p. h.; _____ each at _____ ft. altitude.

Climb: To _____ ft. alt. in _____ min.; rate _____ ft./min. at _____ ft. altitude.

Service ceilings: Normal load _____ ft.; max. bomb/fuel load _____ ft.; min. fuel/no bombs _____ ft.

Fuel: { U. S. gal.: Normal _____ ; max. _____ Take-off, in calm air _____ ft.

{ Imp. gal.: Normal _____ ; max. _____ Take-off, over 50 ft. obstacle _____ ft.

RANGES

Speeds	With Normal Fuel/Bomb Load U. S. gal. and _____ lb. bombs	With Max. Bomb Load and _____ U. S. gal.	With Max. Fuel Load and _____ lb. Bombs
Economical cruising speed	_____ miles	_____ miles	@150mph–3500/ _____ miles
Normal cruising speed	_____ miles	_____ miles	__4500__ miles
Maximum continuous speed	_____ miles	_____ miles	_____ miles
*Typical tactical speeds	_____ miles	_____ miles	_____ miles

*Ref.: p. 4. Pars. 2.

POWER PLANT

No. engines __6__ , rated 1595 / 1495 hp., each at 4,000 / 17,750 ft. alt., with 2700 / 2700 r. p. m. and 38.15 / 38.15 in. Hg.

Description __BMW 801A, 14 cylinder, twin-row, fan-assisted, air-cooled radial.__

Specifications	Supercharger	Propeller	Fuel
Bore __6.14__ in. Dry Wgt. __2960__ lbs.	No. Speeds __2__	Mfr. _____	Rating __87__ octane
Stroke __6.14__ in. Red. Gear __.541__	No. Stages _____	No. Blades __3__	Inlet System: __Direct__
Displ. __2550__ cu. in. Eng. Diam. __52__ in.	Ratios __5.07; 7.47__	Diam. __ ft., __ in. _____	__injection__
Comp. Ratio __6.5__ Eng. Length __58__ in.	Impeller Diam. __13.25__ in.	Pitch Control _____	

ARMAMENT

(F—fixed. M—free.)

(All Free)

For'd fuselage __1 x 13/15/20mm__

For'd wings _____

Through hub _____

Dorsal __2 x 15/20mm__

Lateral __Probably numerous__

Ventral __7.9mm.__

Tail _____

BOMB/FREIGHT LOAD

Normal load _____ kg., _____ lb.

Max. load _____ kg., _____ lb.

Typical stowage _____

_____

Alternate stowage _____

_____

Freight __(est)__ __45,000__ lb.

Troops __Up to 116 men.__

ARMOR

Frontal _____

Windshield _____

Pilot's seat _____

Dorsal _____

Lateral _____

Ventral _____

Bulkhead _____

Engine _____

SPECIFICATIONS

Materials __Metal.__

Span __150'-10½"__ Length __121'-4"__ Height __18'-4"__ Gross wing area __(est) 1400 sq.__ Tail span _____ ft.

Weights: Landing _____ lb.; normal load __Up to 120,000__ lb.; max. load _____ lb.

ADDITIONAL TECHNICAL DATA

At least one turret is believed to be hydraulically-operated. One version is known to have Bramo Fafnir 323 engines and Jumo 207, 6 cylinder, opposed-piston diesels have been reported. Another version is said to have a DB 605 engine in the fuselage to drive a compressor and feed the wing engines.

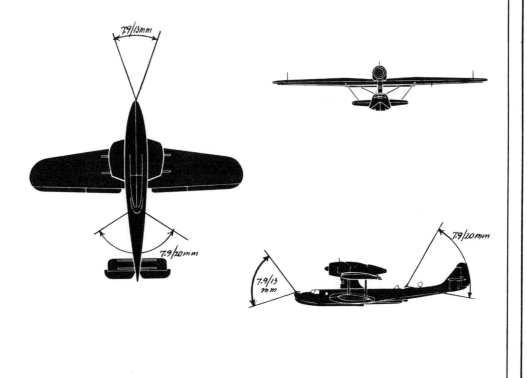

DO 18L

DESCRIPTION

The Do 18L is an older type of flying boat.

It is a twin-engine, braced-parasol monoplane flying boat. Wing center section is carried above hull by faired-in superstructure. Outer-panels taper slightly to rounded tips and are braced to lateral sponsons by parallel struts. Auxiliary airfoil surfaces below and behind trailing edge act as ailerons and flaps. All-metal hull is of semi-circular section with a "V" bottom forward, flattening in region of first step. There are longitudinal steps on each side of keel. The hull is stressed for catapulting, and the stabilizer is braced. The tractor and pusher engine installation is above the wing.

DO 18L

TWIN-ENGINE FLYING BOAT

Mfr. __DORNIER__   Crew __FOUR__

Duty __RECONNAISSANCE.__

PERFORMANCE

Max. emergency speeds _____ m. p. h. @ S. L.; __180__ m. p. h. @ __11,500__ ft. alt.; _____ m. p. h. @ _____ ft.alt.

Max. continuous speeds _____ m. p. h. @ S. L.; _____ m. p. h. @ _____ ft. alt.; _____ m. p. h. @ _____ ft. alt.

Cruising speeds: Normal __154__ m. p. h.; economical __135__ m. p. h.; each at __11,000__ ft. altitude.

Climb: To __11,000__ ft. alt. in __30__ min.; rate _____ ft./min. at _____ ft. altitude.

Service ceilings: Normal load __17,000__ ft.; max. bomb/fuel load __13,000__ ft.; min. fuel/no bombs __20,000__ ft.

Fuel: { U. S. gal.: Normal __(est) 1039__ ; max. _____ Take-off, in calm air _____ ft.

{ Imp. gal.: Normal __(est) 1252__ ; max. _____ Take-off, over 50 ft. obstacle _____ ft.

RANGES

Speeds	With Normal Fuel/Bomb Load __1039__ U. S. gal. and _____ lb. bombs	With Max. Bomb Load and _____ U. S. gal.	With Max. Fuel Load and __1,100__ lb. Bombs
Economical cruising speed	@ __135 mph - 1745__ miles	_____ miles	@110mph -2640 miles
Normal cruising speed	@ __154 mph - 1690__ miles	_____ miles	@132mph - 2450 miles
Maximum continuous speed	_____ miles	_____ miles	_____ miles
* Typical tactical speeds	_____ miles	_____ miles	_____ miles

*Ref.: p. 4. Para. 2.

POWER PLANT

No. engines __2__, rated { 830 / 900 } hp., each at __9,000__ ft. alt., with Take-off { 2450 / 2450 } r. p. m. and { 39.02 / 39.02 } in. Hg.

Description __BMW 132N, 9 cylinder, air-cooled radials in tandem.__

Specifications	Supercharger	Propeller	Fuel
Bore __6.12__ in. Dry Wgt. __1150__ lbs.	No. Speeds __1__	Mfr. __V.D.M.__	Rating __87__ octane
Stroke __6.37__ in. Red. Gear __.620__	No. Stages _____	No. Blades __3__	Inlet System: __Direct__
Displ. __1690__ cu. in. Eng. Diam. __54.5__ in.	Ratios __10.14__	Diam. __ ft.,__ in.	__injection.__
Comp. Ratio __6.9__ Eng. Length __49.5__ in.	Impeller Diam. __9.92__ in.	Pitch Control _____	

ARMAMENT

(F—fixed.   M—free.)

For'd fuselage __1 x 7.9/13mm (M)__

For'd wings _____

Through hub _____

Dorsal __1 x 7.9/13/15/20mm__

Lateral _____ (M)

Ventral _____

Tail _____

BOMB/FREIGHT LOAD

Normal load __200__ kg., __440__ lb.

Max. load __500__ kg., __1100__ lb.

Typical stowage _____

__4 x 110 lbs.__

Alternate stowage _____

Freight _____ lb.

Troops _____

ARMOR

__None__

Frontal _____

Windshield _____

Pilot's seat _____

Dorsal _____

Lateral _____

Ventral _____

Bulkhead _____

Engine _____

SPECIFICATIONS

Materials __Metal, fabric-covering.__

Span __77'-8"__ Length __63'-1"__ Height __17'-10"__ Gross wing area __1,055 sq. ft.__ Tail span _____

Weights: Landing __14,500__ lb.; normal load __18,750__ lb.; max. load __22,050__ lb.

ADDITIONAL TECHNICAL DATA

Hull stressed for catapulting. Radiators for both engines in streamlined structure between wing and tail. Bomb carriers beneath wing. At least one hydraulically-operated turret is fitted on certain sub-types. Front engines drives propeller direct; rear engine drives propeller through a shaft. Earlier versions had Jumo 205C diesel engines, 700 h.p. each @ S.L., giving reduced performance.

DO 24

DESCRIPTION

    The Do 24 flying boat was originally designed and produced for export. A number of these aircraft are still in service, some with Jumo diesel engines and some with BMW 132 air-cooled radials.

    It is a three-engine, parasol-wing monoplane. The engines are supported by the center section of the wing, which is mounted above the hull on inverted-Vee struts. This section is braced to sponsons by sloping parallel struts. Outer sections taper. Split flaps and slotted ailerons are fitted. The shallow hull is the two-step type with the rear step fairing into vertical knife-edge. There are twin fins and rudders at extremities of braced stabilizer. Fuel tanks are carried in the sponsons.

DO 24

THREE-ENGINE FLYING BOAT

Mfr. **DORNIER**   Crew **FIVE TO SIX**

Duty **RECONNAISSANCE. SEA RESCUE. BOMBING.**

PERFORMANCE

Max. emergency speeds **190** m. p. h. @ S. L.; **210** m. p. h. @ **10,000** ft. alt.; _____ m. p. h. @ _____ ft.alt.
Max. continuous speeds _____ m. p. h. @ S. L.; _____ m. p. h. @ _____ ft. alt.; _____ m. p. h. @ _____ ft. alt.
Cruising speeds: Normal **180** m. p. h.; economical **135** m. p. h.; _____ each at **10,000** ft. altitude.
Climb: To **10,000** ft. alt. in **10.5** min.; rate _____ ft./min. at _____ ft. altitude.
Service ceilings: Normal load **21,500** ft.; max. bomb/fuel load **20,500** ft.; min. fuel/no bombs **27,500** ft.
Fuel: { U. S. gal.: Normal **1193** ; max. _____ Take-off, in calm air _____ ft.
{ Imp. gal.: Normal **990** ; max. _____ Take-off, over 50 ft. obstacle _____ ft.

RANGES

Speeds	With Normal Fuel/Bomb Load **1193** U. S. gal. and _____ lb. bombs	With Max. Fgt. Load and **886** U. S. gal.	With Max. Fuel Load and **1320** lb. Bombs
Economical cruising speed	@ **135 mph – 1800** miles	@**135mph–1,250** miles	@**135mph–1710** miles
Normal cruising speed	@ **180 mph – 1485** miles	@**172mph–1,035** miles	@**174mph–1430** miles
Maximum continuous speed	_____ miles	_____ miles	_____ miles
*Typical tactical speeds	_____ miles	_____ miles	_____ miles

*Ref.: p. 4. Para. 2.

POWER PLANT

No. engines **3** , rated **870** hp., each at **8,200** ft. alt., with _____ r. p. m. and _____ in. Hg.

Description **BMW 132Dc, 9 cylinder, air-cooled radial.**

Specifications	Supercharger	Propeller	Fuel
Bore **6.12** in. Dry Wgt. **1150** lbs.	No. Speeds **1**	Mfr. _____	Rating **87** octane
Stroke **6.37** in. Red. Gear **.620**	No. Stages _____	No. Blades **3**	Inlet System: **Direct**
Displ. **1690** cu. in. Eng. Diam. **54.5** in.	Ratios **10.14**	Diam. _ ft., _ in.	**injection**
Comp. Ratio **6.9** Eng. Length **49.5** in.	Impeller Diam. **9.92** in.	Pitch Control _____	

ARMAMENT

(F—fixed.   M—free.)

For'd fuselage **1 free gun**
_____
For'd wings _____
_____
Through hub _____
Dorsal **Turret, 1 x 20mm (M)**
Lateral _____
Ventral _____
Tail **2 x 7.9mm (M)**

BOMB/FREIGHT LOAD

Normal load **600** kg. **(est) 1320** lb.
Max. load _____ kg., _____ lb.
Typical stowage
(est) 12 x 110 lbs.
_____
Alternate stowage _____
_____
_____
Freight **3300** lb.
Troops _____

ARMOR

None

Frontal _____
Windshield _____
Pilot's seat _____

Dorsal _____
Lateral _____
Ventral _____
Bulkhead _____
Engine _____

SPECIFICATIONS

Materials **Metal.**

Span **88'-7"** Length **72'-2"** Height **17'-10"** Gross wing area **1,160 sq.ft.** Tail span _____

Weights: Landing **22,250** lb.; normal load **29,700** lb.; max. load **30,800** lb.

ADDITIONAL TECHNICAL DATA

Turrets may be power-operated. Bomb carriers under wing. Rockets reported for assisting take-off.
If Bramo Fafnir 323R engines of 940 h.p. each at 12,000 ft. are fitted the figures would be slightly
increased; alternatively, with Jumo 205 diesel engines of 700 h.p. @ S.L. the performance would be
slightly lower.

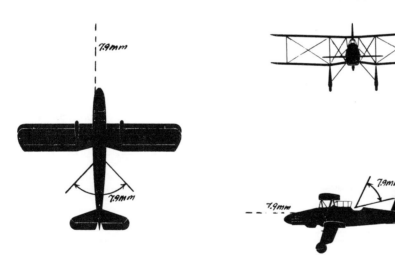

FI 167

DESCRIPTION

The Fi 167 is of an original design which is now obsolescent.

It is a single-engine biplane. Interplane "N" struts are fitted. Wings' outer sections fold. Upper and lower wings both have automatic slots and ailerons, slotted flaps on lower wings. The fixed landing gear is jettisonable for emergency landings on water. There are tandem semi-inclosed cockpits. The stabilizer is braced.

FI 167

SINGLE-ENGINE, CARRIER-BORNE RECONNAISSANCE

Mfr. **FIESELER**   Crew **TWO**

Duty **RECONNAISSANCE. POSSIBLY TORPEDO-DROPPING AND BOMBING.**

PERFORMANCE

Max. emergency speeds **177** m. p. h. @ S. L.; **205** m. p. h. @ **15,000** ft. alt.; _____ m. p. h. @ _____ ft.alt.

Max. continuous speeds _____ m. p. h. @ S. L.; _____ m. p. h. @ _____ ft. alt.; _____ m. p. h. @ _____ ft. alt.

Cruising speeds: Normal **172** m. p. h.; economical **130** m. p. h.; each at **15,000** ft. altitude.

Climb: To **15,000** ft. alt. in **10** min.; rate _____ ft./min. at _____ ft. altitude.

Service ceilings: Normal load **25,000** ft.; max. bomb/fuel load **22,000** ft.; min. fuel/no bombs **33,000** ft.

Fuel: { U. S. gal.: Normal _____; max. **(est) 345** Take-off, in calm air _____ ft.

{ Imp. gal.: Normal _____; max. **(est) 286** Take-off, over 50 ft. obstacle _____ ft.

RANGES

Speeds	With Normal Fuel/Bomb Load **345** U. S. gal. and **1,100** lb. bombs	With Max. Bomb Load and **345** U. S. gal.	With Max. Fuel Load and _____ lb. Bombs
Economical cruising speed	@ **130 mph - 1,120** miles	@**135 mph-1060** miles	_____ miles
Normal cruising speed	@ **172 mph - 940** miles	@**170mph - 930** miles	_____ miles
Maximum continuous speed	_____ miles	_____ miles	_____ miles
*Typical tactical speeds	_____ miles	_____ miles	_____ miles

*Ref.: p. 4. Para. 2.

POWER PLANT

No. engines **1**, rated **1270** hp., each at **16,250** ft. alt., with **2600** r. p. m. and **41.04** in. Hg.

Description **DB 601N, 12 cylinder, liquid-cooled, inverted "V".**

Specifications	Supercharger	Propeller	Fuel
Bore **5.9** in. Dry Wgt. **1400** lbs.	No. Speeds **1**	Mfr. **V.D.M.**	Rating **100** octane
Stroke **6.3** in. Red. Gear **.645**	No. Stages _____	No. Blades **3**	Inlet System: **Direct**
Displ. **2070** cu. in. Eng. Diam. **29.1** in.	Ratios **10.39**	Diam. ___ ft., ___ in.	**injection**
Comp. Ratio **8.2** Eng. Length **67.7** in.	Impeller Diam. **10.23** in.	Pitch Control _____	

ARMAMENT

(F—fixed.   M—free.)

For'd fuselage **1 x 7.9mm (F)**

For'd wings _____

Through hub _____

Dorsal **1 x 7.9mm (M)**

Lateral _____

Ventral _____

Tail _____

BOMB/FREIGHT LOAD

Normal load **500** kg., **1,100** lb.

Max. load **1,000** kg., **2,200** lb.

Typical stowage **4 x 550 lbs.**

Alternate stowage **2 x 1100 lbs.**

4 x 110 lbs.

Torpedo, 1 x 1628/1980 lbs.

Freight _____ lb.

Troops _____

ARMOR

None

Frontal _____

Windshield _____

Pilot's seat _____

Dorsal _____

Lateral _____

Ventral _____

Bulkhead _____

Engine _____

SPECIFICATIONS

Materials **Metal, stressed skin.**

Span **44'-4"**   Length **37'-5"**   Height _____   Gross wing area **490 sq. ft.**   Tail span _____

Weights: Landing **6,800** lb.;   normal load **10,000** lb.;   max. load **11,200** lb.

ADDITIONAL TECHNICAL DATA

Radiator is underslung. Carrier for torpedo or heavy bomb under fuselage. Wing carriers for

4 x 110 lb. bombs. At least one version has DB 601B and lower performance.

HE 115

DESCRIPTION

The He 115 is obsolescent but appears to be in service in limited numbers.

It is a twin-engine, mid-wing monoplane with twin floats. Wing center section is rectangular; leading edges of outer sections are sharply-tapered with detachable round tips. Trailing edge flaps are fitted between ailerons and fuselage. Nose is transparent as is long cockpit inclosure. There is a single fin and rudder of angular shape; stabilizer is braced. Twin floats are of the single-step type, mounted under engine nacelles and attached by "N" struts.

HE 115

TWIN-ENGINE FLOATPLANE

Mfr. **HEINKEL**   Crew **THREE**

Duty **RECONNAISSANCE. BOMBING. MINE-LAYING. TORPEDO-DROPPING.**

PERFORMANCE

Max. emergency speeds **185** m. p. h. @ S. L.; _____ m. p. h. @ _____ ft. alt.; _____ m. p. h. @ _____ ft.alt.
Max. continuous speeds _____ m. p. h. @ S. L.; _____ m. p. h. @ _____ ft. alt.; _____ m. p. h. @ _____ ft. alt.
Cruising speeds: Normal **163** m. p. h.; economical **140** m. p. h.; each at **10,000** ft. altitude.
Climb: To **10,000** ft. alt. in **16** min.; rate _____ ft./min. at _____ ft. altitude.
Service ceilings: Normal load **18,500** ft.; max. bomb/fuel load _____ ft.; min. fuel/no bombs **27,000** ft.
Fuel: { U. S. gal.: Normal **904** ; max. **1060** Take-off, in calm air _____ ft.
{ Imp. gal.: Normal **750** ; max. **880** Take-off, over 50 ft. obstacle _____ ft.

RANGES

Speeds	With Normal Fuel/Bomb Load **904** U. S. gal. and **1,100** lb. bombs	With Max. Bomb Load and **904** U. S. gal.	With Max. Fuel Load and _____ lb. Bombs
Economical cruising speed	@ **140** mph – **1610** miles	@**138** mph–**1590** miles	@**140**mph–**1800** miles
Normal cruising speed	@ **163** mph – **1480** miles	@**161** mph–**1430** miles	@**163**mph–**1660** miles
Maximum continuous speed	_____ miles	_____ miles	_____ miles
*Typical tactical speeds	_____ miles	_____ miles	_____ miles

*Ref.: p. 4. Para. 2.

POWER PLANT

No. engines **2** , rated **920** hp., each at **2,000** ft. alt., with _____ r. p. m. and _____ in. Hg.

Description **BMW 132K, 9 cylinder, air-cooled radial.**

Specifications	Supercharger	Propeller	Fuel
Bore **6.12** in. Dry Wgt. **1150** lbs.	No. Speeds **1**	Mfr. **V.D.M.**	Rating **87** octane
Stroke **6.37** in. Red. Gear **.720**	No. Stages _____	No. Blades **3**	Inlet System: **Direct**
Displ. **1690** cu. in. Eng. Diam. **54.5** in.	Ratios **7.0**	Diam. ___ ft., ___ in.	**injection**
Comp. Ratio **6.9** Eng. Length **49.5** in.	Impeller Diam. **9.92** in.	Pitch Control _____	

ARMAMENT

(F—fixed. M—free.)

For'd fuselage **1 x 7.9 + 1 x 15 mm (F)**
wings aft. **2 x 7.9mm (F) in engine nacelles.**
Through hub _____
Dorsal **1 x 7.9mm (M)**
Lateral _____
Ventral _____
Tail _____

BOMB/FREIGHT LOAD

Normal load **500** kg., **1,100** lb.
Max. load **910** kg., **2,020** lb.
Typical stowage **Internal**

1 x 1100 lbs.
Alternate stowage **1 mine**
Torpedo, 1 x 1650 lbs.

Freight _____ lb.
Troops _____

ARMOR

Frontal _____
Windshield _____
Pilot's seat **15mm**

Dorsal _____
Lateral _____
Ventral _____
Bulkhead _____

Engine _____

SPECIFICATIONS

Materials **Metal, stressed skin.**

Span **72'-6"**   Length **56'-8"**   Height **21'-7"**   Gross wing area **942 sq. ft.**   Tail span _____

Weights: Landing **15,800** lb.; normal load **23,500** lb.; max. load **24,200** lb.

ADDITIONAL TECHNICAL DATA

Floats can be fitted with "skates" for landing on ice.

DESCRIPTION

Mfr._____ Crew_____

Duty_____

PERFORMANCE

Max. emergency speeds_____ m. p. h. @ S. L.;_____ m. p. h. @_____ ft. alt.;_____ m. p. h. @_____ ft.alt.

Max. continuous speeds_____ m. p. h. @ S. L.;_____ m. p. h. @_____ ft. alt.;_____ m. p. h. @_____ ft. alt.

Cruising speeds: Normal_____ m. p. h.; ____ economical_____ m. p. h.;____ each at_____ ft. altitude.

Climb: To_____ ft. alt. in_____ min.; rate_____ ft./min. at_____ ft. altitude.

Service ceilings: Normal load_____ ft.; max. bomb/fuel load_____ ft.; min. fuel/no bombs_____ ft.

Fuel: { U. S. gal.: Normal_____ ; max._____ Take-off, in calm air_____ ft.

{ Imp. gal.: Normal_____ ; max._____ Take-off, over 50 ft. obstacle_____ ft.

RANGES

Speeds	With Normal Fuel/Bomb Load _____ U. S. gal. and _____ lb. bombs	With Max. Bomb Load and _____ U. S. gal.	With Max. Fuel Load and _____ lb. Bombs
Economical cruising speed	_____ miles	_____ miles	_____ miles
Normal cruising speed	_____ miles	_____ miles	_____ miles
Maximum continuous speed	_____ miles	_____ miles	_____ miles
*Typical tactical speeds	_____ miles	_____ miles	_____ miles

*Ref.: p. 4. Para. 2.

POWER PLANT

No. engines_____ , rated_____ hp., each at_____ ft. alt., with_____ r. p. m. and_____ in. Hg.

Description_____

Specifications
Bore_____ in.
Stroke_____ in.
Displ._____ cu. in.
Comp. Ratio __ :_____

Dry Wgt._____ lbs.
Red. Gear_____ :____
Eng. Diam._____ in.
Eng. Length_____ in.

Supercharger
No. Speeds_____
No. Stages_____
Ratios_____
Impeller Diam._____ in.

Propeller
Mfr._____
No. Blades_____
Diam.____ ft.,____ in._____
Pitch Control_____

Fuel
Rating_____ octane
Inlet System:_____

ARMAMENT

(F—fixed.   M—free.)

For'd fuselage_____
_____
For'd wings_____
Through hub_____
Dorsal_____
Lateral_____
Ventral_____
Tail_____

BOMB/FREIGHT LOAD

Normal load_____ kg.,_____ lb.
Max. load_____ kg.,_____ lb.
Typical stowage_____
_____
Alternate stowage_____
_____
Freight_____ lb.
Troops_____

ARMOR

Frontal_____
Windshield_____
Pilot's seat_____
Dorsal_____
Lateral_____
Ventral_____
Bulkhead_____
_____
Engine_____

SPECIFICATIONS

Materials_____

Span_____ Length_____ Height_____ Gross wing area_____ Tail span_____

Weights: Landing_____ lb.; normal load_____ lb.; max. load_____ lb.

ADDITIONAL TECHNICAL DATA

DFS 230

DESCRIPTION

The DFS 230 is one of the G.A.F.'s standard gliders.

It is a high-wing, braced monoplane. Wing has high aspect ratio and tapers moderately to rounded tips. A single bracing strut is on each side of the fuselage, which is of rectangular cross section. Passengers are seated on boom running down the center of the fuselage. The pilot's cockpit is forward of the wing; some versions have dual control. The cabin door has a quick-release mechanism. There is a single fin and rudder and adjustable stabilizer. Landing skids are employed, as wheeled landing gear is jettisoned for operational flights.

| | DFS 230 | |

| | GLIDER | |

Mfr. **GOTHA** .... Crew **ONE OR TWO**

Duty **TRANSPORT** ....

PERFORMANCE

		T U G			L O A D S			S P E E D S A N D R A N G E S				
Type	No.	Engines	Fuel Tankage U.S. gals		(a) No. of Men (b) Freight lb.		No. of Gliders towed	Cr. Sp mph	Alt. ft.	Climb to Alt. mins.	Range miles	Endurance hours
He 111	1	2 x Jumo 211 F	1134		(a) 10 (b) 2,800		1	110 110 110	S.L. 5,600 10,200	⸺ 8.4 17.3	1,400 1,340 1,230	12.7 12 11.2
He 126	1	Bramo 323 A	136		(a) 10 (b) 2,800		1	110 110	S.L. 4,200	⸺ 6.5	430 430	3.3 3.9
Ju 52	1	3 x BMW 132A	1060		(a) 10 (b) 2,800*		1	100 100 100	S.L. 3,000 6,000	⸺ 7.0 15.0	1,150 1,200 1,100	10 10.2 9.3
Ju 52	1	3 x BMW 132A	1060		(a) 10 (b) 2,800*		2	100 100 100	S.L. 3,000 6,000	⸺ 13.0 25.0	1,100 1,120 1,030	9.4 9.7 8.7
Ju 87	1	Jumo 211 J	362		(a) 10 (b) 2,800		1	110 110 110	S.L. 4,500 7,500	⸺ 6.1 10.6	840 760 790	7.7 7 7.2
Me 110	1	2 x DB 601 N	920		(a) 10 (b) 2,800		1	110 110	S.L. 5,000	⸺ 4.1	1,560 1,420	14.2 12.9

Special remarks: *In addition to glider load, the Ju 52 could carry 2,800 lb. internal load in troops (14 men) or freight.

ARMAMENT

(F—fixed.   M—free.)

For'd fuselage ....
Light machine guns can
For'd wings **be carried.**
....
Through hub ....
Dorsal ....
Lateral ....
Ventral ....
Tail ....

BOMB/FREIGHT LOAD

Normal load .... kg., ... lb.
Max. load .... kg., ... lb.
Typical stowage ....
....
Alternate stowage ....
....
Freight .... **2800** lb.
Troops **10 fully-equipped, incl. 1/2 pilots**

ARMOR

Frontal ....
Windshield ....
Pilot's seat **8mm**
....
Dorsal ....
Lateral ....
Ventral ....
Bulkhead ....
....
Engine ....

SPECIFICATIONS

Materials **Metal tubing, wood, fabric, plywood.** ....

Span **72'-4"** ... Length **37'-6"** ... Height **10'** ... Gross wing area **(est.) 450 sq. ft.** Tail span ....

Weights: Landing **1800** lb.; normal load **4,700** lb.; max. load .... lb.

ADDITIONAL TECHNICAL DATA

Tugs: 1 x He 111, Hs 126, Ju 52, Ju 87, and Me 110. ....

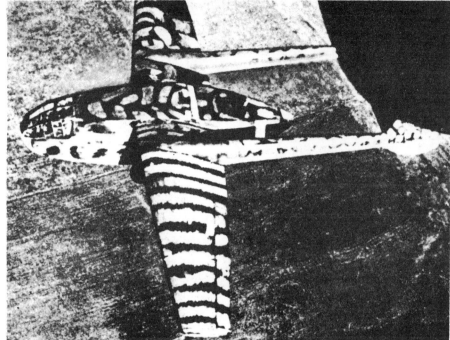

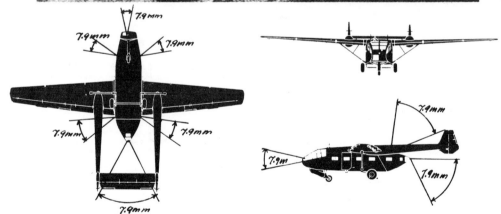

GO 242

DESCRIPTION

The Go 242 is one of the standard German gliders.

It is a high-braced-wing, twin boom monoplane. There is a central nacelle, the rear of which is hinged for loading purposes. Strut-braced wings are tapered, tips square. Flaps and lift spoilers are fitted to the wings. A jettisonable wheeled landing gear is provided, landing being effected on three skids. The central skid is retracted in flight.

GO 242

GLIDER

Mfr. **GOTHA**   Crew **TWO**

Duty **TRANSPORT**

PERFORMANCE

		T U G			L O A D S			S P E E D S A N D R A N G E S				
Type	No.	Engines	Fuel Tankage U.S. gals.		(a) No. of Men (b) Freight lb.	No. of Gliders towed		Cr. Sp mph	Alt. ft.	Climb to Alt. mins.	Range miles	Endurance hours
He 111	1	2 x Jumo 211 F	1140		(a) 23 (b) 5,300	1		149 149 130	S.L. 5,600 10,000	--- 13.8 28.2	1,040 1,030 900	7 7 7.1
Ju 52	1	3 x BMW 132	664		(a) 23 (b) 5,300*	1		112 85	S.L. 3,000	--- 16.7	530 620	4.7 7.3
Me 110	1	2 x DB 601 N	920		(a) 23 (b) 5,300	1		149 149	S.L. 5,000	--- 6.5	1,280 1,210	8.6 7.4

Special remarks: *In addition to glider load, the Ju 52 could carry 2,800 lb. internal load in troops (14 men) or freight.

ARMAMENT

(F—fixed.   M—free.)

For'd fuselage **1/2 x 7.9mm (M)**

For'd wings

Through hub
Dorsal **1 x 7.9mm (M)**
Lateral
Ventral
Tail **1 x 7.9mm (M)**

BOMB/FREIGHT LOAD

Normal load _____ kg., _____ lb.
Max. load _____ kg., _____ lb.
Typical stowage **840 cu. ft.**

Alternate stowage

Freight **5,300** lb.
Troops **23 fully-equipped, incl. 1/2 pilots**

ARMOR

Frontal **5 & 8 mm.**
Windshield
Pilot's seat **8mm sides**   **3mm bottom**
Dorsal
Lateral
Ventral
Bulkhead

Engine

SPECIFICATIONS

Materials **Wood, fabric, plywood, metal tubing.**

Span **79'**   Length **52'-7"**   Height _____   Gross wing area **700 sq. ft.**   Tail span

Weights: Landing **7,200** lb.;   normal load **12,500** lb.;   max. load _____ lb.

ADDITIONAL TECHNICAL DATA

Tugs: 1 x He 111, Ju 52, and Me 110. Arrestor gear is fitted in form of hooks at rear of each

skid, to shorten landing run. Maximum permissible speeds: (1) Towed, 149 mph; (2) Gliding, 180

mph; Minimum gliding speed at S.L. (1) Loaded, 87 mph; (2) Empty, 68 mph.

ME 321

DESCRIPTION

The Me 321 is the largest glider known to be in operation in the G.A.F.

It is a braced, high-wing monoplane. Wings are moderately tapered, tips blunt. The thick fuselage is of the two-deck type, the floor of the upper being detachable to enable motor vehicles to be carried. There is a single fin and rudder. Landing skids and jettisonable landing wheels are provided. The nose consists of two large, rounded doors, through which loading and unloading are normally effected. Numerous emergency exits closed by zip fasteners are in side of fuselage.

ME 321

"GIGANT" GLIDER

Mfr. __MESSERSCHMITT_____ Crew_____

Duty __TRANSPORT_____

PERFORMANCE

				LOADS			SPEEDS AND RANGES				
		T U G									
Type	No.	Engines	Fuel Tankage U.S. gals.	(a) No. of Men (b) Freight lb.		No. of Gliders towed	Cr. Sp mph	Alt. ft.	Climb to Alt. mins	Range miles	Endurance hours
He 111	2	2 x Jumo 211 F	2 x 1140	(a) 130 (b) 26,000		1	140 140 120	S.L. 5,600 10,000	--- 19.3 42.9	950 980 820	6.8 7 6.9
Ju 52	2	3 x BMW 132	2 x 664	(a) 130 (b) 26,000*		1	115 100	S.L. 3,000	--- 22.2	550 550	4.8 5.5
Me 110	2	2 x DB 601 N	2 x 920	(a) 130 (b) 26,000		1	155 155	S.L. 5,000	--- 10.8	1,060 910	6.8 5.9

Special remarks: *In addition to glider load, each Ju 52 tug could carry 2,800 lb. internal load of troops (14 men) or freight.

ARMAMENT

(F—fixed. M—free.)

For'd fuselage_____
_____
For'd wings_____
Through hub_____
Dorsal_____
Lateral __Poss. 6 x 7.9mm (M)_____
Ventral_____
Tail_____

BOMB/FREIGHT LOAD

Normal load_____kg.,_____lb.
Max. load_____kg.,_____lb.
Typical stowage_____
_____2700 cu. ft._____
_____
Alternate stowage_____
_____
_____
Freight _____26,000__ lb.
Troops _130 fully-equipped men._____

ARMOR

Frontal_____
Windshield_____
Pilot's seat __Proably protected.__
_____
Dorsal_____
Lateral_____
Ventral_____
Bulkhead_____
_____
Engine_____

SPECIFICATIONS

Materials __Metal tubing, fabric, plywood._____

Span__181'____ Length__93'-4"___ Height__27'-6"___ Gross wing area __3000 sq.ft.___ Tail span_____

Weights: Landing__24,000____ lb.;   normal load__50,000____ lb.;   max. load_____ lb.

ADDITIONAL TECHNICAL DATA

Tugs: 2 x He 111, Ju 52 and Me 110.

DESCRIPTION

Mfr._____ Crew_____

Duty_____

PERFORMANCE

Max. emergency speeds_____ m. p. h. @ S. L.; _____ m. p. h. @ _____ ft. alt.; _____ m. p. h. @ _____ ft.alt.

Max. continuous speeds_____ m. p. h. @ S. L.; _____ m. p. h. @ _____ ft. alt.; _____ m. p. h. @ _____ ft. alt.

Cruising speeds: Normal_____ m. p. h.; ____ economical _____ m. p. h.; ____ each at_____ ft. altitude.

Climb: To_____ ft. alt. in _____ min.; rate_____ ft./min. at_____ ft. altitude.

Service ceilings: Normal load_____ ft.; max. bomb/fuel load_____ ft.; min. fuel/no bombs_____ ft.

Fuel: {U. S. gal.: Normal_____ ; max._____ Take-off, in calm air_____ ft.

{Imp. gal.: Normal_____ ; max._____ Take-off, over 50 ft. obstacle_____ ft.

RANGES

Speeds	With Normal Fuel/Bomb Load U. S. gal. and_____ lb. bombs	With Max. Bomb Load and_____ U. S. gal.	With Max. Fuel Load and_____ lb. Bombs
Economical cruising speed	_____ miles	_____ miles	_____ miles
Normal cruising speed	_____ miles	_____ miles	_____ miles
Maximum continuous speed	_____ miles	_____ miles	_____ miles
*Typical tactical speeds	_____ miles	_____ miles	_____ miles

*Ref.: p. 4. Para. 2.

POWER PLANT

No. engines_____ , rated_____ hp., each at_____ ft. alt., with_____ r. p. m. and_____ in. Hg.

Description_____

Specifications	**Supercharger**	**Propeller**	**Fuel**
Bore_____ in. Dry Wgt._____ lbs.	No. Speeds_____	Mfr._____	Rating_____ octane
Stroke_____ in. Red. Gear____ : ____	No. Stages_____	No. Blades_____	Inlet System:_____
Displ._____ cu. in. Eng. Diam._____ in.	Ratios_____	Diam.____ ft.,____ in._____	
Comp. Ratio ___ : _____ Eng. Length_____ in.	Impeller Diam._____ in.	Pitch Control_____	

ARMAMENT
(F—fixed.   M—free.)

For'd fuselage_____

_____

For'd wings_____

Through hub_____

Dorsal_____

Lateral_____

Ventral_____

Tail_____

BOMB/FREIGHT LOAD

Normal load_____ kg.,_____ lb.

Max. load_____ kg.,_____ lb.

Typical stowage_____

_____

Alternate stowage_____

Freight_____ lb.

Troops_____

ARMOR

Frontal_____

Windshield_____

Pilot's seat_____

_____

Dorsal_____

Lateral_____

Ventral_____

Bulkhead_____

Engine_____

SPECIFICATIONS

Materials_____

Span_____ Length_____ Height_____ Gross wing area_____ Tail span_____

Weights: Landing_____ lb.; normal load_____ lb.; max. load_____ lb.

ADDITIONAL TECHNICAL DATA

_____

_____

_____

_____

PRINTING
IMPRIMERIE GAGNÉ